RESTORED

From Failure to Faith and Freedom

David Cook

RESTORED

FROM FAILURE TO FAITH AND FREEDOM

DAVID COOK

David Cook

Restored: From Failure to Faith and Freedom by David Cook
Copyright © 2019 by David Cook
All Rights Reserved.
ISBN: 978-1-59755-504-3

Published by: ADVANTAGE BOOKS™
                Longwood, Florida, USA
                www.advbookstore.com

This book and parts thereof may not be reproduced in any form, stored in a retrieval system or transmitted in any form by any means (electronic, mechanical, photocopy, recording or otherwise) without prior written permission of the author, except as provided by United States of America copyright law.

All scripture quotations unless otherwise marked are taken from the KING JAMES VERSION of the Holy Bible: public domain.

Scripture quotations marked CSB are taken from the Christian Standard Bible ®, Copyright © 2017 by Holman Bible Publishers. Used by permission.

Scripture quotations marked AMPCE are taken from the Amplified Bible, Classic Edition, Copyright © 1954, 1958, 1962, 1964, 1965, 1987 by The Lockman Foundation. Used by permission.

Scripture quotations marked ESV are taken from The Holy Bible: English Standard Version, copyright 2001, Wheaton: Good News Publishers. Used by permission. All rights reserved.

Scripture quotations marked The Message are taken from The Message. Copyright © 1993, 1994, 1995, 1996, 2000, 2001, 2002. Used by permission of NavPress Publishing Group.

Library of Congress Catalog Number: 2019935294
Religion: Christian Life - Inspirational

First Printing: May 2019
19 20 21 22 23 24 25   10 9 8 7 6 5 4 3 2 1
Printed in the United States of America

ACKNOWLEDGEMENTS

I want to say a very special thank you to some amazing people who made this project possible. You have each contributed to my life and, subsequently, to this book.

First and foremost, I want to thank my Heavenly Father for sending Jesus to die for me. God has been so good to me, and I am thankful every day for His abounding mercy and His amazing grace! Every blessing in my life has come from Him, and this book was made possible because He enabled me to do it. Thank you, Lord, for all You've done in my life!

To my amazing and beautiful wife Becca: I could not take one step in this life without you. I may never know this side of Heaven why God sent you to me, but I can never be thankful enough. You preach the Gospel to me every single day by simply being by my side. I love you, love our family, and can't wait to see how God works in our lives!

To my children, Nick, Sarah, Ashley and Joseph: I hope that you hear my heart through the pages of this book and realize that I love you all more than I can ever say.

Thank you to my pastor, Dr. Rod Parsley. You are a true father in the faith, and you have been the most consistent voice in the Kingdom in our generation. For over 40 years, you've unashamedly declared the whole counsel of God. You have welcomed us home with open arms, and I'm humbled and honored beyond words for the love you've shown to my family. I respect you, I honor you, and I thank you for the influence you are in my life and my family.

To Elder Bill and Mrs. Paula Canfield: thank you for your encouragement and assistance in editing this book. You have challenged me and been supportive of me all at the same time. I have grown because of your input. With your help, this project took on a crisp, sharp presentation. I am forever grateful for your friendship and guidance.

Thank you, Pastors Randy and Mary Jo Starkey, Pastors Terry and Patti House, and all of the pastoral staff, administrative staff, ministry leaders, and the congregation of Victory Church. I would not be where I am today without you all. Thank you for loving me and my family and accepting us as we were from our very first visit. Regardless of where God takes any of us, we are forever connected!

To Pastor David Baldwin: you were the first pastor to recognize God's calling on my life. You disciplined me, loved me, corrected me, and laughed with me. You gave me opportunities to grow and to learn as a preacher, a leader, a husband, and a father. I'm thankful for your mentorship and friendship in my life. You and your family mean the world to us.

To Pastors John and Debbie Lowe: thank you for always being willing to speak the truth to us, and for accepting us and loving us. You are tremendous pastors and leaders, and we love you all very much. We are honored to know you and serve our King together with you.

To Pastors Brian and Jillian Gallardo: thank you for being our friends and receiving us with open arms. You have played a significant role in me being where I am today, and in completing this book. God brought you to me at a time when I needed a push. You have been a constant encouragement to me over the past few years. We love you dearly.

To Apostle Josphat Ndumbu and Soul Harvest Ministries in Mombasa, Kenya: without a doubt, you are one of the most influential people in my life. I have always felt as though I knew you on a deep level, even the first time we met. Your ministry in Kenya is so far beyond what anyone can imagine. You are truly reaching the unreachable and building the Kingdom of God every day. Your zeal for His work is contagious, and I am so grateful for you. You are a gift to the body of Christ, and to my family.

There are many others who have been such an amazing part of my journey. Time and space would not permit me to thank you all in this format. Please know that I thank God for every pastor, family member and friend who has stood with me, prayed for me, and supported me.

Table of Contents

ACKNOWLEDGEMENTS 5

FOREWORD 11

INTRODUCTION 13

   1: BEGIN WITH THE END IN MIND 15
      The Dawn of a New Day 17
      Reflection 20

   2: A PLAGUE AND A PROCESS 21
      The Plague 22
      The Process 23
      Reflection 24

   3: THE PAST IN THE PRESENT 27
      It Wasn't *About* Me, but It *Affected* Me 27
      Childhood Memories 29
      Attempts to Make Things Better 30
      Why Me? 31
      Attempt to Start Again, Again 32
      Reflection 33

   4: GOING DEEPER—IT'S GENERATIONAL 35
      My Dad's History 35
      On into My Family 36
      Reflection 39

   5: A PINHOLE OPENING 41
      Fear = Pride 42
      The Struggle for Validation 43
      Reflection 45

   6: THE PINHOLE WIDENS 47
      Pinholes Popping Everywhere 50
      Reflection 52

7: LIVING IN THE FOG 55
The Fog of War 55
Loss of Vision 56
Reflection 60

8: NOW THE FLOOD 63
The Spiritual Swamplands 63
Floating in Flood Water 66
Reflection 69

9: LICKING UP EVERY SCRAP 71
A Culture of Fear and Failure 72
I Hurt, So I Have to Hurt 74
Reflection 76

10: DEVASTATED AND DEVOURED 77
Completely Cut Off 80
Unsuccessfully Seeking Success 80
The Strength of Joy 81
Reflection 82

11: TURN AND REPENT 85
Naked and Ashamed 85
My Turn 88
Reflection 89

12: REVERSE YOUR COURSE 91
The Means to Serve Him 92
We Need Relationships to Survive 94
Reconnection 96
Reflection 99

13: ORDERLY RESTORATION 101
A New Covenant 101
Reflection 105

14: RESTORING VISION 107
Looking for a Common Goal 108
Pioneering Spirit 108

But Wait …There's More 110
God's Desire to Partner with Us 111
Reflection 112

15: RESTORING PROVISION, PROTECTION AND PRIVACY 115
Man of Many Masks..116
It Has to Change 118
Reflection 119

16: RESTORING FREEDOM 121
The Caterpillar Is Losing Its Grip 121
It Just Doesn't Fit Anymore 123
Reflection 125

17: SEALING THE WORK 129
Time to Move 130
What Consumed Me Will Sustain Me 132
It's Coming Fast 133
Reflection 134

18: A SPIRIT OF ADOPTION 135
Using What I Know 136
Meeting Myself in Joseph 137
Reflection 141

19: PROGRESSING IN FAITH 143
Roadblocks..143
Behavior Explained 145
Change Is in the Air 145
Reflection 147

20: TIME TO TESTIFY 149
Back to the Beginning 150
Time Is Accelerating 151
He WILL Provide 152
Everything Is Ready—Now the Answer Can Come 153
Reflection 156

FOREWORD

I met David Cook –an extraordinary man—when he was a young Marine. He was given to two things in life: his family and the Corps. The dedication to his family has always been a testimony to those who know him. Although life has given David some rough challenges, he has always been ready to acknowledge and repair the pain he endured, leaving it behind. He is a restored man, a mature man—a man who has enjoyed the love, acceptance and forgiveness of God, his family, and those who care deeply for him. That is why he can write this fine work on restoration.

David is like a son to me. In our relationship, as he has shared with me, his level of honesty and forthrightness was always refreshing. David is a man of God who is ready to convey to the reader the freedom of restoration and the joy of taking back what the enemy has stolen.

As you read the pages of his book, you will find yourself thinking and praying about your own life, and how you, too, can find eternal freedom.

Pastor Dave Baldwin
Moyock Assembly of God
Moyock, North Carolina

David Cook

INTRODUCTION

When I was in high school, I had a good friend who restored a classic car. He and his father worked diligently on that car, hoping that it would be ready for him to drive when he turned sixteen. The car was a mid-1960s Ford Mustang.

They were able to clean up and use some of the original parts of the car, while some parts had to be purchased from salvage yards, and some parts had to be purchased new. The restored car, once it was finished, had the best of the old mingled with the best of the new. When the car was ready to drive, it was in better shape than it had been in its original state.

We have all faced challenging times in life when a temporary failure sets us back a step or two on our journey toward our dream or our calling in the Lord. But then there are those times when we have really blown it and failed—a full-on, no-holds-barred, fouled-it-up, and may-never-recover-from-it kind of failure!

Failure can be life-altering. Like a knockout blow, it can put us down on the mat where we can't even lift our head toward the Heavens to pray.

Failure happens for many reasons. Sometimes there are external factors, over which we have no control, but other times, it is our own fault, and we simply blow it with God.

Failure can be the result of generational issues in our family. In Exodus 20:5, the Bible says that the sins and iniquities of the fathers will be visited to the third and fourth generations. There may be curses in families from generations before, and unless someone breaks that curse through faith in Jesus Christ, it will continue throughout the family lineage. However, there's hope!

For years, I've had a picture hanging in my child's room of a father praying by his son's bedside. Underneath the picture is James 5:16. It reads: "*The effectual fervent prayer of a righteous man availeth much.*" The cycle of sin in our families CAN be broken through the power of the Holy Spirit operating in our life.

Failure is not a foreign experience to most, but restoration to right standing with God can be a difficult concept to grasp when we are in such a place. The road to restoration can be very long and very difficult; however, it is not impossible. Thank God, we are on this side of grace! I believe our God is a God of restoration! The message of the Cross is a message of restoration. Jesus came to pave a path of restored fellowship with the Father. We are now able to come boldly before Him and have fellowship with Him.

In Joel 2:25, God says, "*And I will restore to you the years....*" When I consider this passage of scripture, I believe it is referring to more than just the years that were lost in my lifetime.

The Ford Mustang my friend restored was from the mid-1960s. He was born in 1971, and he restored it in the mid-1980s. That car had been broken-down for a generation before my friend ever started working on it!

When God restores, He restores ALL that was taken from you, whether it was in your lifetime or not. I'm not talking about money or possessions, although those things could be a part of it. I'm talking about positional, relational, physical, and emotional restoration. I am talking about being restored to your rightful place through Christ. I am talking about dominion, which was lost by Adam, but taken back by Jesus! The restoration of dominion in your life will bring about restoration in every area of your life.

May the pages that follow convict your heart to turn toward Him, no matter what condition you find yourself in today. May they stir you to seek His face more than ever. May the power of the Holy Spirit invade your life today, and every day, and bring healing to your heart, to your family, and to all that concerns you. God bless you as you read the story of my journey from failure to restoration, and may the grace, mercy and favor of our Lord lead you to higher heights in Him!

1

BEGIN WITH THE END IN MIND

The congregation applauded as I approached the platform. My palms were sweating, and my heart felt as if it were going to jump out of my chest. My knees were trembling, and every fiber of my being was shaking. I had tears in my eyes as I put my Bible and iPad on the podium and looked up at the people who were waiting to hear a word from God. I don't know if anyone in the room, other than the pastor of the church and my family, realized how significant this moment was to me. I had been out of the pulpit for a very long time.

Leading up to this moment were a long series of events—events which had brought me to the lowest point in my life, from which I was certain I could never recover. This book is the process of my journey into and out of that place of utter failure and defeat and into the position of recovery and restoration.

During the month of April 2017, my wife and I were on a weekend trip to Kansas City, Missouri, with our daughter Sarah, and Joseph, the little boy we were trying to adopt. We planned to visit some friends on Saturday and spend some time with a pastor I knew from Bible college on Sunday. We were visiting some attractions around the city, and had just left the Truman Library and were headed downtown to visit Union Station. My phone rang as we were driving; it was a pastor I knew in Indiana. He and I had met several years before, but I had lost contact with him until we reconnected in 2016.

After the pleasantries and greetings were out of the way, he said, "I am having a leadership training event at my church on August 5, 2017. I want you and your wife to come, all expenses paid." I responded, "Well, I will have to check the calendar. I am the head football coach, and that's our first day of full-contact practice. I have never missed one since I took over the program."

He responded, "I don't think you understand, brother. God *told* me to have you come. I want you to come, and it won't cost you a thing. AND, I want you to spend the night and preach for me on Sunday."

The phone went silent for a few seconds, which felt like an eternity. My wife was looking at me out of the corner of her eye and smiling at me the entire time I was on the phone. I think she could either hear the conversation, or she had some inclination of what we were talking about. I told him, "Pastor, I need to make sure I can make it work. Can I talk to my wife and get back to you?"

He said, "Sure. But I'm telling you, this is what the Lord spoke to me. I want you to come to the leadership event, and then preach for us on Sunday."

By the time I parked my car in downtown Kansas City, I had told Becca what the pastor had said. She looked at me and replied, "You're going to do it. I believe this is from the Lord."

I called my friend back and said to him, "Pastor, my wife said I'm going to do it. I'll come. I will even stay over and preach for you. Are you sure you want me to?"

Again, a few more seconds of awkward silence, and then he said, "Well, that was easier than I expected! I thought I'd have to work a little harder to get you to agree!" That Saturday afternoon, I began preparing for a time of ministry to come some four months later.

We were able to work things out so I could get my practices in with the football team. I had approached our school administration, our athletic director, and our coaching staff to figure out a plan. We decided to have what we called Midnight Madness at 12:01 a.m. on August 5, 2017. Our team, then, was among the first football teams in the entire state to have their first full-contact practice for the season. I walked in the door of my home after the practice at 3:00 a.m. I slept about two hours, then loaded the car to drive to Indiana.

We arrived at the church in Indiana just in time for the start of the leadership event. It was a great time, and I had the opportunity to meet some wonderful people. We worked in small groups and discussed a variety of leadership topics. Most of the core leaders in the church were present that day, and I'm not sure they had any idea of why I was there, aside from being a friend of their pastor.

That evening, after we had dinner with the pastor and his wife, we went to our hotel room to get some rest. Even though I was exhausted from a tough week of practices with my team and the lack of sleep from the night before, I couldn't sleep. I kept going over my notes and poring over the passages of scripture the Lord had put on my heart for the next day. I was even praying and questioning God, saying, "Are you sure, God? Did you really call me to do this? Is this the message you want me to deliver?"

I was too nervous to sleep, but too tired to focus. I just sat there, asking God to give me peace about this and help me rest. After several hours of tossing and turning, reading and praying, I finally dozed off to sleep.

The Dawn of a New Day

It was early in the morning on August 6, 2017, and we were just waking up in our hotel room in this small town in southwestern Indiana. Two of our children, Nicholas and Sarah, were with us, but our youngest daughter, Ashley, was at home because of her work schedule. Shortly after I got out of bed, I sent her a text telling her how I would have loved for her to be here, too, but hoped she would be able to follow us via social media throughout the day. It meant the world to me to have my wife and children together for the service that morning.

The weather was cloudy and unusually cool for that time of year. As I stood in the hotel room looking out the window, my heart fluttering in my chest, I could not help but wonder, how did I get here? How did all of this come together and culminate at this point in my life? Will anyone want to hear what I have to say? Will it help anyone? I knew, beyond a shadow of a doubt, that I was not worthy to do what I was about to do.

We ate breakfast, loaded the car and headed to the church where I would be preaching that morning. This was the first time I would stand in a pulpit and deliver the Word of the Lord since 2003. For fourteen years, I had said that I would never preach again, and now I was running headlong right back to it. We stopped at a local coffee shop, then continued on to the church.

As I walked into that building that day, I was as nervous as a man about to watch his bride walk down the aisle. I tried to sit down and be still, but I just couldn't. I had to walk around and move.

The service began with some great praise and worship music. I wept as the worship team led the congregation in songs of praise and worship to our God. I felt my wife's hand on my back throughout the beginning portion of the service, and I knew she was praying for me.

My son had helped me develop slides as an illustration for my sermon that day. I had studied and prepared so diligently, but every possible scenario I could think of was running through my head—things like, "What if the slides don't work? What if the anointing isn't on this? What if I stumble over my words? What if I can't speak at all? What if they don't receive it? What if I'm wrong? What if the pastor missed it, and I'm not supposed to be here?"

The final song the worship team did that day was a song about restoration. I sensed the presence of the Holy Spirit as they sang about God's power and willingness to restore broken people. The title of my message that day was "Restoring the Years."

The pastor went to the platform and began the transition portion of the service. He received the weekly tithes and offerings and proceeded to introduce me. I had visited the church one other time, and he had introduced me to the church then, but this time was different. He told the congregation, "This man has a word from God. He is my friend, and God is doing a work in his life, and is restoring him. Please welcome my friend, Brother David Cook, as he comes to share the Word of God with us today."

As the congregation applauded, and I took the platform—my heart pounding and my mind racing—the magnitude of what I was about to do weighed heavily on my heart and mind. I recall thinking to myself, "Lord, you have placed these people's lives into my hands today." The influence of the pulpit is heavy, and the direction of their lives could be altered or changed forever based on what I was about to say.

So, I began to deliver the message. The sermon I was preaching today was the very last one I had preached in 2003. God had shown me something in Joel about how the enemy takes, and how God restores. In fact, it was even the same title. I had come full circle to get to this point.

I was rusty and unpolished, but I poured out my heart for 60 minutes. By most standards, that's at least 20-30 minutes too long, but the people were gracious and allowed me to get it all out. As I drew close to the end of the message, I looked at the pastor and said, "I'm not sure how to end this, but can I pray for people?"

He said, "Of course!" I gave an altar call for those who felt like they needed to be restored in some area of their life, whether it was in their ministry, their church or their family—whether financially, relationally, emotionally, or any

Chapter 1: Begin With The End In Mind

other way. In that small church, we had 12 people respond and come to the altar. I wept as I walked to each one and prayed that God would heal their hearts, their minds and their bodies, and would seal His word in their lives.

After I was finished, the pastor shared a prophetic word for us that he had received several months earlier. He said, "You are coming back, but this time it will be more powerful than you imagined."

He told my wife, "You are the one who held all of this together, and you will be a witness to many people of how God restored you and your husband, and your ministry." He shared some other insights he had received from the Lord about my children, then he prayed for us and ended the service.

One man came up to me after the service with tears streaming down his face and said, "I needed this so badly! I've strayed away from the Lord, and He brought me here today. I didn't know why I wanted to come to church today, but I did, and I'm thankful that I did." I wept with him, and we prayed together again before he left the auditorium.

As I left that building, I felt such a sense of relief, but I was also struggling in my mind. The pastor hadn't given me a time limit, but had I preached too long? Had I included things I shouldn't have, or had I excluded things I should have included? Had I been too transparent? This service was on Facebook Live, and I was tagged in the video post, so I was not sure who would see it or what they might think. We had not told anyone of our desire to re-enter the ministry, other than the pastors of our local church and a couple of very close friends.

That evening, after we got back home, we had an event at our local church. We walked in the door, and one of our associate pastors said to me, "Well, now we know you can preach!"

I had really been hoping that no one would have seen or heard it. I looked at my Facebook page, and a friend of mine from high school had commented on the post, affirming me and stating how it had ministered to them. Although I was critiquing myself, God still used it to minister to people.

Over the course of the next few days, as I processed each of these things in my mind, I began to find the peace of God in each question I had about that day. I remembered how much I used to love ministering God's word! I loved preaching and teaching. It was not that I enjoyed being in front of the crowd, it was that I enjoyed digging into the word of God through study and prayer, and pulling out a message that could change lives.

Reflection

God told Adam and Eve in the Garden of Eden that they could eat anything, from any tree they wanted, except for one—the tree of the knowledge of good and evil (Genesis 2:16-17). They did eat from that tree, as we know, and sin entered the world. Even though God's plan had been that man would live without sin, He also had a plan that would allow them to be restored when they did sin. When Adam sinned, the plan of God to restore mankind to right fellowship with Him was already settled and in place—the Lamb of God had been slain from before the foundation of the earth (Rev 13:8).

The same is true for us today. He has a plan for us to obey, but He has a plan for when we don't. The message of restoration is very personal to me, as I have lived it over the past fourteen years. When I first saw this concept in Joel 1 and 2, I really believed that God was talking to me about what we had already experienced in ministry. I had no idea that my life was going to spiral downward at a rapid pace. But God has a plan: even from the beginning, He has an end in mind.

2

A PLAGUE AND A PROCESS

I was serving as an associate pastor of a church in Western Ohio in 2003. Every day on the way to and from the church, I passed by fields full of rows and rows of corn. That summer, I spent several days studying Joel 1 and 2. One Wednesday afternoon in June, as I was preparing for a youth service that evening, I began to sense something in this passage that stopped me in my tracks. There was just something about it that I could not get past. I started to dig into the Word of God, using every commentary, dictionary, and translation I had at my disposal.

As I studied and pored over Joel 1, I saw so many profound points that related to what I had faced the previous five years. Joel was describing an army that was coming toward Judah, and the destruction that would be left in its wake. It appeared that the armies advancing through Judah were like an enormous plague of locusts that left the land depleted. I felt that I could identify with this. Our time in ministry, up to that point, had been riddled with problems. We had faced one attack after another, as they came against us in wave after wave!

The more I studied this passage, the more I concluded that Joel was describing both a plague and a process. Joel was describing failure and restoration, and the process of both.

About a month later, I was scheduled to preach the weekend services. I felt that I had a word from the Lord, so I put together an outline and prepared to preach a sermon I titled, "Restoring the Years." The church responded to the message, and God ministered to several people that morning.

However, I had no idea what was coming, or what I was about to walk through over the next fourteen years. I did not realize what my family would endure, or that I would reach an all-time low in my life. I believed in 2003 that we were on the edge of a miracle in our family, our marriage, our ministry and our finances.

The Plague

Joel uses four distinct terms to describe the army besieging Judah. In Joel 1:4, he uses the following words to describe the adversaries as a plague of locusts:

- Palmerworm – Gnawing Locust
- Locust – Swarming Locust
- Cankerworm – Licking Locust
- Caterpillar – Consuming Locust

In the study of scripture, there are some guiding principles that will help us understand what God is saying. One of those principles is the *law of first mention*. The law of first mention means that in order to understand a biblical truth, we want to pay particular attention to the order in which things are named or listed in scripture. Therefore, it is reasonable to conclude that there is a reason why the Bible lists things in a particular order.

I have read many commentaries and listened to a number of scholars present their ideas about this passage in the book of Joel. Some believe the words used here describe the actual stages of development within the *same* swarm of insects, while others believe the Joel is referring to *different* swarms of locusts at varying stages of development.

The reality of what Joel is describing here is an army that is coming, like a plague of locusts, to devour the land of Judah. The people to whom Joel was prophesying understood locusts. They had, at the very least, heard or read about the plagues of Egypt when God sent locusts on the land. They had undoubtedly experienced locusts in their fields and around their territories. The language is descriptive and written in a way that the people could understand.

As I read through this passage and studied every single word, I began to see how the enemy of my soul had come against me. The eyes of my heart were opened that afternoon in my small home office, and God was revealing His Word to me in a way I had never seen before.

I jumped over to Joel 2 and started looking at the scriptures about restoration. Like most people, I wanted to avoid the process of development and skip right to the blessing. I remember thinking as I read through the chapter, "Man, that will preach! I have to get this in an outline now!"

The problem with viewing this simply as a plague of locusts that came from some unknown source or for some unforeseen reason is that it frees us from any personal responsibility. I may be tempted to believe that this is a fact of nature, beyond my natural control. I might buy into the notion that someone else did wrong, and I had nothing to offer concerning a solution, nor was there any blame to lay on my shoulders. Therefore, all I had to do was cry out to God in desperation, and He would hear me and deliver me from this unwarranted attack. Viewing this passage as a plague only would then free me from any personal responsibility, the need for action, or a call to repentance.

The Process

The more I studied Joel 1 and 2, the more I saw that it was not only a plague, but it was also a process. There is a process to everything in this life and in the earth. For example, if we dig a hole in the ground, put a seed in it, and care for the soil with water and fertilizer, over time the seed will grow and produce a harvest. Although this is a very simplified description, it is the process of farming.

There are a few observations I made concerning the advancement of Judah's enemy as Joel described it. First, I found that several commentaries suggest a variety of reasons why Joel lists the locusts in Joel 1:4 in a certain order. Some commentators believed that it was the same army—the same plague of locusts—coming back to Judah again and again. If that were the case, at least in a depictive manner, the locusts were coming, consuming, leaving, developing and returning. However, this is contrary to what we know about locusts. They do not return to an area once they have devoured it. Therefore, this destruction had to have come from multiple advancements by different armies over time.

Secondly, in the United States, some regions will experience swarms of locusts about every 13-17 years. Therefore, we may conclude from Joel that the attack was calculated months, maybe even years, in advance. In the context of Joel's prophecy, when the worm or caterpillar burst forth from the egg, the march was on. It is possible that the locust was already in the land, or close to it, and the people had no clue it was there. Like spies, the enemy was lying in wait for the right season to attack.

Thirdly, as the first group of locusts did their damage, the next swarm —

which was a bit farther along in their development—came, until through wave after wave, all available resources were consumed, and the people were left defenseless, exposed and uncovered.

Finally, locusts generally come from the south. However, in this passage, Joel describes the armies of the attacking nations as coming in from the north. The attack came as a surprise to the slumbering nation, and from a direction they were not anticipating. They were not well-defended in the direction of the advancing enemies.

There were blind spots in the land of Judah that were not covered; the same thing was happening in my life. There were areas of weakness in Judah that had been ignored or unnoticed for a long time, because nothing ever really came from that direction. It didn't happen overnight: it had been developing for years, and it came from a place they were not expecting. I began to see that there were areas of my life that had been left uncovered. Generations of sin that had plagued my family before I was ever thought of were lying at the door, waiting for me. The attacks came from places I didn't expect, and from directions where I was not even paying attention.

In reviewing the terms used in this descriptive passage of Scripture, there is a definitive process to failure. As I studied each word, in light of the supporting passages throughout Joel 1 and 2, it became evident that the people of Judah had become content and complacent, and in some cases, had even turned their back on their God. In turning away, they left areas open, exposed and unchecked.

Reflection

There is a process for everything in life. There is a process for farming, a process to earn money, a process to reproduce, and a process to grow – physically, emotionally, and spiritually. As a football coach, I tried to teach my players to commit to the process of the game. I taught them not to worry about the scoreboard in the first quarter; just stay focused on the process of the game. Then, as you get closer to the end of the game—if your plan was solid, if you gave all you had in the tank to offer—you will have given yourself a chance to win. It's a process.

If there is a process to win, there must also be a process to fail. In our instantaneous society, we do not understand the process. We have information at our fingertips twenty-four hours a day. We can find out about anything or anyone on the World Wide Web. Nothing is hidden, nothing is private, and everything is instant. Today's generation struggles with committing to the process of life, work, education, and ministry.

We must be wise concerning our enemies' devices. The devil does not attack us from the front, and he will not fight us in an area of strength. He will attack us in the most vulnerable places—when we have let our guard down, and when we least expect it. In the pages ahead, I'm going to explain how this process played out in my life and how God has used it to bring about miraculous healing and restoration in my life and family.

Sometimes the challenges we face are not of our own doing, but they become our battle because of the actions of others. But praise be to God, if we are in Christ, the fight isn't ours, but the Lord's! He has won the victory, and He has given us power over all the forces of the adversary!

David Cook

3

THE PAST IN THE PRESENT

One of my teachers once said, "What's fair isn't always equal, and what's equal isn't always fair." Regardless of how your life experiences measure up to someone else's, the truth of the matter is that your life is your own. To move forward, you must come to terms with your past, regardless of whether your experiences were negative or positive: fair isn't equal, and equal isn't fair.

As we consider our struggles and battles in light of Joel 1:4, it is important to notice the order of the locusts listed in his prophecy: "*That which the palmerworm hath left hath the locust eaten; and that which the locust hath left hath the cankerworm eaten; and that which the cankerworm hath left hath the caterpiller eaten.*"

The first one mentioned is the palmerworm. A palmerworm is a *gnawing insect* which, at certain stages of its life, comes together in a swarm, devouring all the green plants in its path. This insect represents those things that gnaw at our spirit, our soul, and perhaps even our physical bodies until there is an opening through which they can flood our lives with destruction. Sometimes, we have no control over the things that gnaw at us.

Our life experiences, if not appropriately covered under the blood of Christ, can leave openings for the adversary to attack. From my experience, this begins in the mind. We have to master our thought life, or we will continually struggle with the same things.

My present life is a direct reflection of all that has happened before I got to this point in time. I never fully realized it until God began a new work in me in 2014. Some things happened in my family before I was born, and when I was very young, that created openings for the devil to step in. There were circumstances in the past over which I had no control that shaped both the present and the future of a small, impressionable boy.

It Wasn't *About* Me, but It *Affected* Me

It was a warm, Saturday afternoon in the spring of 1981. I was about to turn ten years old. We were living in a small town just west of St. Louis,

Missouri. Our home was a rental, with two bedrooms, one bathroom, and a small basement.

The morning began with an argument between my parents. This had been going on for at least a couple of days, but on this particular day, it was more heated than ever. This was not the first time I had heard them fighting, but something about this day seemed different. This argument seemed more serious and the words I heard cut deeper than anything I'd heard before. There was a sense of finality this time.

I walked into the hallway and watched my mom as she pulled my dad's clothes out of the closet and threw them out of the room. She even took some scissors and began cutting up some of his clothing. I can't remember all that was said, but I do recall the screaming and the yelling, and how harsh the exchange was.

My grandmother, who lived with us until I was 15, sent me to a friend's house down the hill that day. Although I tried to play and ride my bike with my friend, I could still hear the fighting and yelling coming from our little rental house just up the hill.

A few hours later, I ran back up the hill. As I came around the corner of our house, I watched my dad take a coffee mug—one that I had made for him—off the dashboard of his car, and throw it at our front door. As it shattered all over the ground, he cursed at my mother and drove off. When he was gone, I went around to the front of the house and cleaned up the broken mug. I threw the pieces in the garbage and went inside to get something to eat.

About an hour later, he came back to the house and knocked on the front door. I recall being baffled by the notion that he knocked on the door of his own home. My mother opened the door, and he came in and sat down on the couch. He looked toward the kitchen where I was sitting with my grandmother and said, "I just came back here so I could kill you all!"

I jumped up and ran out the back door, and that's the last thing I can remember about that day.

A few months later, my mom moved us closer to her family. That year, I started school in the 5th grade, and was in that same school district until I graduated from high school. She filed for divorce, and we started a new life without him.

Chapter 3: The Past in the Present

Childhood Memories

When I was a child, my mother and father were never together. Even in the early days of their marriage, and throughout their life together, my dad would get up in the middle of the night and leave our house. He would stay gone for days—sometimes months—at a time.

My mother told me that altogether, he left us about sixty times. Sometimes, he was only gone for a day or two, and other times, he would stay gone for much longer. My grandmother on my mother's side stayed with us off and on until I was fifteen years old. In my dad's absence, she helped take care of me.

My dad made it known to my mother shortly after I was born that he didn't want a family at all, and most certainly wanted nothing to do with me. My mother told me that when I was just a few days old, he had said, "Either that kid goes, or I go!" He would say that, and then leave.

Growing up, I remember hearing him make this and similar statements to me. I wondered why he felt this way. As a child, I could not understand it. I thought there must be something wrong with me. As an adult, I got to the point where I expected it.

My mother told me that during the ten years they were married, we moved over twenty times. We lived all over the state of Missouri, looking for the next break. My dad was a bit of a beggar, but he was a likable person at first. He would always find ways to meet people, then he'd wear out his welcome, get mad at people, and we would move.

I can recall holidays and birthdays sitting around waiting for my dad to show up. He would make empty promises and never follow through on any of them. Birthdays and holidays were emotional roller coasters for me. I would start the day so full of hope and excitement thinking that he'd actually come this time, only to be disappointed when he didn't even bother to call.

Because of his choices, there were times in our life when we had to take food stamps and public assistance. I know there are others who had it much worse than I did, but it made a strong impression on my young mind and heart. Poverty became a genuine fear for me going into adulthood.

As a kid, I was sick a lot. One school year, I had strep throat five times. I was anemic and had an iron deficiency, which carried over to some degree into adulthood. My hearing was poor due to multiple infections in my ears. Thankfully, I had a surgery to correct that when I was nine years old.

After my mom and dad divorced, we moved back to my mother's hometown. Life then became simple, but challenging. For some time after we moved back there, we lived in an old cinder block house where the roof leaked, and we had a wood stove for heat. There was an addition put on the back of the house, adding an indoor bathroom and another bedroom. In the winter, the water pipes under the addition in the back would freeze and break, and we'd have to fill a trash can with water at my uncle's house and use that to drink, cook, and bathe until the pipes were repaired.

Throughout my childhood, my mother never owned a home, and she always drove an older car. Somehow, though, she always managed to maintain a roof over our heads and put food on the table. We had times of lack and want, but we managed. It wasn't easy, and I know she struggled, but she did what was needed to take care of me.

Attempts to Make Things Better

When I was twelve years old, my mother remarried. Through their short marriage, the man maintained contact with his two previous wives, and was emotionally abusive to my mother.

On the surface, we seemed to be doing better. We were building a home, which I worked on and learned how to do a few things related to construction. It was an A-frame house, and I put the upper floor ceiling trusses together and raised them by myself.

However, the whole situation was just wrong. The man promised me that if I worked with him to build the home, he would buy me a car when I turned sixteen. It was an empty promise: we never lived in that home, and he never helped me get a car. About nine months into the marriage, he moved me and my mother into an old trailer and left us there to live with his previous wife. He moved his first wife into the house and lived there with her until he passed away several years later.

While we were living there in that trailer park, I watched my mother break down emotionally. I still believe to this day that she either had, or was very close to having, a nervous breakdown and should have been hospitalized. My grandmother was staying with my uncle at the time, and I was there with my mom alone at the age of thirteen and didn't know how to help.

About a year after her second husband left her, my mom met another man and remarried again. Throughout their four-year marriage, he was physically abusive to her. He tried to abuse me, but by this time, I was a sophomore in high school and had no concerns about holding my own. When I did stand up for myself, he'd kick me out of the house. As a result, from time to time throughout high school, I had to stay with friends, or even one of my coaches.

My mother's third husband had two children from his first marriage, and there were issues with both of them. His son would periodically use drugs and make threats about things he was going to do. At one point, he said he was going to attack me in my sleep. I wasn't afraid of him, nor of my step-father, but I slept with a baseball bat in my bed and my back as close to the wall as I could get it for the three years we lived there. I remember nights I would wake up with that bat in my hand, ready to swing away at anyone or anything that came in the room.

Why Me?

Growing up I could not understand why everyone else's family seemed to be so healthy, but mine was such a mess. I can remember asking God, "Why me? What did I do to deserve this mess?" I felt isolated and alone, even though there were people around me and friends and community members who cared for me. I couldn't understand it or come to terms with it. I began to believe there must be something inherently wrong with me if my father wanted nothing to do with me, and that I'd never be able to have a stable family and life. It seemed as though the father-figures in my life felt the need to exert their power over me and over my mother—and they did so successfully.

The threats and abusive behaviors toward me were not a result or consequence of bad behavior on my part. I was not a bad kid and never got into trouble, or had any issues with the police. I had decent grades and attended school regularly. I was never a straight A student, but I did well in school. I wasn't on drugs, and I didn't run around to parties. I kept company with the people I played sports with, and we stayed out of trouble. Of course, there were times we did some stupid stuff—none of us were saints.

David Cook

Attempt to Start Again, Again

After I graduated from high school and moved off to college, things got worse for my mother. I was trying to put all of this behind me and make my own way. I thought I could overcome all of my family history and prove my worth through hard work, athletics and education. I found myself reeling in college, trying to keep up. By the time I was in my third semester, I was on academic probation. My goal was not to earn a degree but rather to find acceptance in some group somewhere.

I came home the summer after my sophomore year in college and found my mother with a black eye, and clumps of hair pulled out. Her third husband had punched her in the face, slapped her, and dragged her through the house by the hair of her head. That summer was awful. He and I had a fist fight, and I went to stay elsewhere. About a year later, I joined the Marine Corps.

By May of 1992, my mom had finally had enough and left him. She moved into another trailer park, where she purchased a mobile home, just south of where she had been living. That dilapidated old mobile home was the first residential property she ever owned.

She remarried again in 1994, this time to a man who was much older than she was. They lived in that old trailer until he passed away in 2009. After that, she moved into a small apartment just a few miles away, and sold the old trailer.

In 2011, she remarried again. I only wish she had met this man twenty years earlier! He has treated her very well. She has a home to call her own—a real house, not a mobile home, and she has a brand-new car for the first time in her life.

As a result of the lifestyle she chose to live, we bounced around a lot from the time I was born, until I was in the 5th grade. There were many people in and out of our lives, the majority of whom at least claimed to be Christians. We attended conservative, denominational churches, but I never saw the results of what I heard there demonstrated in my life or in my home. I guess I questioned—or maybe doubted—what the churches I attended as a child taught me.

The decisions we make can have lasting effects on our children. My family history is checkered at best, yet I do not think anyone was trying to give me a bad start in life. I never knew anything different concerning family life, other than what I experienced at my friends' homes, saw on television, or read about in books or magazines. I had no real understanding of what a real family looked like or what being a man truly meant.

Reflection

My dad couldn't read or write; my mom dropped out of high school to start working. The fact that neither parent had much formal education seemed to leave a deep impression on me. I hated the way my life was as a child, and I wanted to do everything I could to change it forever.

Over the years, the devil *gnawed* at me with that thought. Every time I hit a wall, or faced a struggle, I was reminded of what my life had been like as a child. I had a prideful desire to overcome all of that in my own strength.

Like the *gnawing* of the palmerworm, the *gnawing* of our past can undoubtedly affect our present. In my case, the things that went on in my family when I was a child had a profound impact on me as an adult. For a while, I felt as if I had come to terms with it—even sharing bits and pieces about my upbringing with some very close friends. Until later in life, I never really knew exactly how deep the wounds were.

The *gnawing* of the palmerworm will keep at your soul until there is a large enough opening there to gain a better hold on you. It is so important to take "*...every thought captive to the obedience of Christ*" (2 Corinthians 10:5). The longer we ponder our failures, the longer we ponder our less-than-desirable pedigree, the longer we ponder how much we want to be something other than what we are, the larger the hole the palmerworm can make to do his destructive work in our lives.

David Cook

4

GOING DEEPER—IT'S GENERATIONAL

The challenge facing the land of Judah in Joel 1 was not something that came about overnight. It was more than the invasion of a conquering army; it was the continuation of a cycle of defeat and victory that had happened over and over again throughout their history. Joel not only asks the older generation if they or their ancestors have ever seen anything like this but also admonishes his readers to tell their children and their grandchildren about it. Joel is presenting a generational message that transcends the limitations of time. Both the previous generations and the ones to come are urged to remember and learn from the current conflict.

In my own life, I can look at the things that happened in previous generations and see how they influenced my life today. I can also look at whatever it is I am going through and see how it might influence the lives of my children in the future.

My Dad's History

Over the past few years, I have learned quite a bit about my dad's upbringing. He was the youngest of three children by the same mother and father, with one brother and one sister. Their father left them when my dad was only a few days old. My grandfather had other children by other women, and my grandmother remarried multiple times.

My dad most likely had a mental illness or possibly a neurological disorder of some type. Had he been born two generations later, I suspect he and his siblings would have been placed in foster care, and he would have received special education services at school. There are indications that he was molested when he was around twelve, although I do not know for certain. What I do know is that he had significant challenges in his life that made him the person that he was.

He never finished school and never accomplished much of anything. He could neither read nor write, and he lived most of his life as a beggar, bouncing around from place to place. My aunt and I talked many times about what would become of him, and we hoped that we would at least be able to give him the dignity of a proper burial at the end of his life.

He was always in and out of church, trying to prove he had received some miracle from God. Oddly enough, he was even a pastor for a short time at a small church just south of St. Louis. I have some memories of that little church, and I recall my mother reading the scriptures for him when he would preach, as he was unable to do so himself. The church did grow, and we had several young families in attendance during our short tenure there.

He was also secretly into crossdressing. When I was 19, he told me he wanted to have gender reassignment surgery, so he could live out his life as a woman. In retrospect, I recall instances where he engaged in this behavior while he and my mother were still married. I do not understand how any of us made it out of that stage of our lives.

My dad was challenging to talk with. Most of the time, he was unfocused on anything or anyone other than himself. I felt as though I never really knew him. I always had a soft spot for him in my heart, but I wanted nothing to do with the lifestyle he lived, nor did I want to be anything like him.

The more I learn about my family history, the more I realize that God placed something in my heart that told me this was not the way a man should live, nor is it how God intended for families to exist. However, this troubled me on into adulthood. I was convinced that I was meant to struggle in every area of my life. I believed that no matter what I tried, I'd always be pulled down by my family history.

On into My Family

In 1992, I began dating the most amazing woman I have ever met. Becca's smile lights up a room, and her positive outlook is a tremendous blessing to me.

We were married in 1993. We began our life together in Jacksonville, North Carolina, where I was stationed at Camp Lejeune in the United States Marine Corps. We started attending a great church there, and I rededicated my life to Christ on Christmas Eve, 1993. I remember weeping like a child as our pastor stood there and prayed with me.

I later shared with the pastor that I felt the Lord had called me to preach. He started mentoring me and working with me. I even did some preaching there

Chapter 4: Going Deeper – It's Generational

on Wednesday nights, and volunteered as their youth leader. In 1995, I got out of the Marine Corps, and we decided to move to Columbus, Ohio, where I would attend Bible college.

One Sunday, a man named Gary approached me as we were leaving church. He said, "I see God's call on your life, son. I have set up a scholarship out of my home church in Florida to pay your way through Bible college. All tuition, fees, books, pens, paper, typewriter—whatever you need."

I knew who Gary was before this, and we had exchanged greetings a few times, but that was the first real conversation we ever had. After that, we regularly talked by phone. I even had the opportunity to visit and minister in the church in Florida where the scholarship was set up.

Gary passed away from cancer in 1998, which was a major blow to me. I still miss him. Whatever I do for the Kingdom, it is all because Gary believed in God's calling on my life. I look forward to the day when we reunite in Heaven.

By the time we left North Carolina to move to Ohio, our son, Nicholas, had been born. Just before we left North Carolina, a car hit us from behind while at a stop light. As a result of the medical exam following the accident, we learned that my wife was pregnant with our second child, Sarah. It was scary. But we felt like God had called us, protected us, and would provide for us. So, we did the unthinkable: we moved to a place we'd never been, where we didn't know a soul, and where I didn't even have a job.

I was supposed to receive my final pay the day we left Camp Lejeune, in November of 1995. We planned to use this money to pay our final utility bills and cover moving expenses. When I went to the administration office on base to pick up my pay, they handed me a check for about one-tenth of what I was supposed to receive.

The government had shut down that morning, due to gridlock between Congress and the President over the national budget, and full payment was going to be delayed. We had already mailed out our bills that morning and finalized our plans to move. I had to make an advance payment on storage space in Ohio and rent a moving truck. The money was already spoken for.

Of course, we panicked like never before! I started adding up the cost for all of the returned check fees that we would be facing. We called as many of our creditors as possible and pleaded with them to hold off on depositing our payments until we could get the money deposited to cover them. Nearly all of them said there was nothing they could do.

I recall feeling physically sick during the two-day drive from North Carolina to Ohio, to the point where I couldn't even eat. This was not the way I thought I would be feeling on my way to Bible college!

We were planning to spend the coming Thanksgiving holiday with family in St. Louis. First, though, I was going to drop Becca and the baby off at the airport in Columbus, where they were booked on a flight to St. Louis. I was going to stay in Columbus for a few days to look for an apartment and a job, then I was going to join them. When we got to Columbus, I drove our seventeen-foot moving truck with a vehicle trailer attached to the back through the airport drop-off lane, so I could let my pregnant wife and eight-month-old son out to catch the plane to St. Louis. It was quite a sight!

We didn't have cell phones or any other way to communicate until we both reached our destinations. I didn't even know where I was going to stay that night. I drove my moving van over to the east side of Columbus and found the cheapest hotel room I could find. I went inside, sat down on the bed, and cried. My wife and baby were on a plane, on their way to visit our family. I was alone in Columbus, where I didn't know a single person, sitting in a hotel. We were facing a significant financial challenge, and I had no idea how it would come together.

This wasn't the first time I felt like this, but I recall hearing that gnawing litany in my mind about how I would end up no better than my father. I couldn't provide for my wife and son and my unborn daughter. *Why even try? Why was I here? What was I hoping to accomplish?* The enemy of my soul bombarded my mind over the next few days until I couldn't think straight.

The following Sunday morning, I went to the church where I'd be attending Bible College. I had $25 cash in my pocket, and I felt like the Lord spoke to my heart that morning to give it in the offering—so I did. When I got back to my hotel room later that day, I learned that the government shutdown was over, and all delayed payments would be issued that very next week. I called my wife and told her the news. We were so grateful for an answer to our prayers, and I'm confident the prayers of many other families affected by the shutdown.

I stayed on in Columbus for the next few days, looking for an apartment and a job. I set up some appointments to meet with a couple of leasing agents after Thanksgiving. I had a few job interviews scheduled. I was able to store all our belongings in a storage unit, so I headed to St. Louis a week before Thanksgiving to join everyone for the holiday. We planned to return to Columbus the next week to set up our apartment.

Reflection

In my adult life, I've had a number of negative interactions with my dad in which he would become angry, turn on me, and disown me. The last time was in 2005. I was going to school full time to finish my bachelor's degree, and I was working two jobs to take care of our family. He got mad because I did not want to come and get him out of the hospital. He told me I was never his son, and that I was now dead to him. I had heard this all before.

We are not always able to identify the actions of the enemy in our lives, or recognize right away that it is him at work. Some of the situations he created in my life began before I was even born, and many were while I was still a small child—they had nothing to do with me. However, all the things I saw and heard took root in my heart. Even though I thought I was over them, I was not.

Before 2014, I had not sufficiently dealt with the depth of the wounds in my own heart and mind. I was bound by the fear of failing as a husband, failing as a father, and failing as a man. I was always seeking the approval of others. I felt inferior to my peers, and even to my wife.

I wanted so badly to be a son. I craved the bond that is shared between a father and a son. As an adult, I battled with sin and felt like I didn't deserve anything good in life. I felt like I was just meant to struggle. I was terrified of failure. The palmerworm had gnawed away at my sense of self-worth and left me feeling alone and defeated.

The words used to describe the attacking army coming against Judah may well be descriptive of locusts in various stages of development. If you think about the span of time between locust invasions, particularly in America, you are talking about 13-15 years. As I look back over my life, I can see that the enemy's calculated, well-placed attacks were meant to take me out. A few times, he nearly won! Had it not been for the Lord on my side, who knows what might have become of me?

It is crucial to our spiritual health that we put our whole life on the altar. Having good relationships, especially with father figures and mentors, is vital. We need to make sure we are connected with those who will not only cover us and love us unconditionally, but who will also call us out on our mistakes and restore us. If we don't experience this in our families, we can look to God and we can trust him to make up for what we lack or what we missed out on.

What experiences have taken place in your life that opened the door to the adversary? Perhaps it was something that happened to you—maybe you were abused. Maybe you were molested. Maybe your family has a history of alcohol or drug addiction. Maybe your family was riddled with all types of sin. Perhaps you were alone. Perhaps you were abandoned. Whatever it was, God can restore the years—even the years that you missed. God can reverse it all and restore life to your family and your descendants!

5

A PINHOLE OPENING

"Keep your feet moving! Keep driving forward!" As a high school football coach, I always told my running backs to keep their feet moving and to keep driving, so that the defenders could not bring them down with a shoestring tackle or a foothold. Several things can go wrong when you stop moving your feet and legs, such as fumbles or injuries. I always told them not to plant their feet in the ground and push but rather keep moving.

After a tackle, the ball is always placed at the spot where forward progress ended. I knew that as long as they stayed in motion, it was less likely that the defense could stop them from gaining ground, and we would maximize our gains and keep moving toward the end zone.

Ephesians 4:27 says, *"Neither give place to the devil."* The smallest entry can allow things to seep into your life, thus giving the enemy a foothold on you—a tackle that will take you to the ground.

The palmerworm, or gnawing locusts, is the first army mentioned in Joel 1:4. This army represents the little things, the small sins, that we allow to gnaw at our spiritual health. Perhaps it is pride. Perhaps it is fear. Perhaps it is financial mismanagement. Or maybe it's just a combination of things that have built up over time. When we give place to the devil, we allow him room to gnaw away at our relationship with God.

Sin always starts small, and it always begins in the mind, where it grows and festers. You begin obsessing over it. You can't get away from it. It begins to consume your thoughts, and before long, you start acting on those thoughts. Sin grows, little by little. The devil only needs a pinhole opening to start his work.

Satan and his demons cannot create anything. He himself is a created being. Therefore, he can only manipulate us in our flesh. James told us to resist the devil and he will run from us in terror (James 4:7). Paul told the church at Ephesus to put on the whole armor of God and stand firm (Ephesians 6:11). When we allow ourselves to be exposed in weakness to anyone other than

Christ and those He places in our lives to encourage us, we are entering dangerous territory.

Two of the most powerful forces in life are love and fear. Love is a tremendous motivator. Love is what drives people to do extraordinary things to care for others. Fear is also a tremendous motivator. Fear can be rational or irrational. Rational fear helps us avoid dangerous situations, but irrational fear can cripple us, as it did me most of my life.

Although it looked like I was taking great steps of faith, in reality, I was afraid. I was afraid of ending up like either one of my parents, or even worse. When my wife and I were married in 1993, I told her, "I don't know how to do this. I don't know how to be a husband or a parent. All I know is that I shouldn't leave you, but I don't know how to treat you."

Fear = Pride

For the better part of my life, I was afraid of being poor, and I was afraid of failing as a husband and father. We lived in poverty to some degree as I was growing up, and I certainly saw what failing as a husband and father looked like. I remember being embarrassed about the conditions of my life, and feared ever having to put my family through that.

I was afraid of failing my wife and kids. For most of my adult life, I felt like I was constantly looking over my shoulder, waiting for failure to overtake me. I was fearful of making mistakes, taking the wrong course in life, or just not being very good at this husband and dad thing. I recall hitting difficult points in my life and making statements like, "I'll never be able to get past this. It works for everyone but me. I must just be cursed." This was my default response, and I struggled to understand how God could ever love me, or have need of me, in His Kingdom business.

Fear drives us into disagreement with God's Word. To disagree with His Word is to disagree with Him. God and His Word are one. John 1:1-2 says, *"In the beginning was the Word, and the Word was with God, and the Word was God. The same was in the beginning with God."* John 1:14 also says, *"And the Word was made flesh, and dwelt among us, (and we beheld his glory, the glory as of the only begotten of the Father,) full of grace and truth."*

The Bible tells us that God is love, and perfect love drives out all fear (1 John

4:16; 1 John 4:18). If we want to drive away fear, we must come into agreement with His Word. We must receive His love and realize that to Him, we ARE worth the price He paid for us! Neither our sin, our past, nor our family history is greater than His sacrifice on Calvary's cruel cross.

I allowed pride to enter my life, and that was a key component on my road to failure. Fear is the opposite of faith. Therefore, fear is disobedience to God and has its roots in pride. In other words, when we are fearful, we are saying that *we* are in control.

The reality is that God is in control. It is not up to us to make things happen. He only asks that we believe. Hebrews 11:6 says, *"...without faith it is impossible to please him...."* Faith is scary to our flesh. However, when our faith is based on the Word of God, we can let go of our fear and fully trust Him.

The Struggle for Validation

Proverbs 16:18 says this, *"Pride goeth before destruction, and an haughty spirit before a fall."* We have all seen ministries and ministers fail. In some of these cases, there is a visible sin that is exposed, and the news media—and even the Church—eats them alive. I didn't have a major moral failure while serving in ministry, but what happened to me is certainly no better or worse than the sins we have seen so many Christian leaders engage in.

I would argue that they probably began their path to failure in very much the same way I did. In some cases, people begin feeling as though they are invincible and impervious to sin and its effects. In other instances, people tend to be afraid of letting God do a work in and through them in His timing. Either way, pride is at the root of all sin. Remember, Satan said, "I will be like God" (Isaiah 14:14), which meant he could neither sin nor fail. This is nothing more than pride.

In Mark 10, a man came to Jesus asking what he must do to have eternal life. Jesus told him that he must keep all the commandments. The man answered that he had kept all of them from the time he was young. What Jesus says next is a hard thing. He told the man to sell all that he had, give the money to the poor, and follow Him.

The scripture says that the man walked away, and his countenance changed. He became gloomy and was saddened by this because he had a lot of possessions. He had hoped that Jesus would see how successful he was, and that he was a good man who followed all the rules. He had obviously come to Jesus prepared to do more good works in order to earn eternal life. He came to Jesus with an attitude of pride, and Jesus responded with a requirement that was tough for him to swallow.

After I graduated from Bible College in 1998, we set out to pastor a small church in Western Ohio. I felt like I had some ministry experience, and had certainly been well-trained in Bible College. In most of the challenges I faced early on, I may not have known the answer, but I knew where to look for them.

When I started in ministry, I had a big vision and a big dream. I wanted to do so much for God, and I truly believe in my heart that was my motivation. However, I got so wrapped up in the "superstar mentality" that I felt I had to meet the right people and make the right connections on my own to make it happen. I was always adamant about telling others about the remarkable things we were doing in ministry, in the hopes that someone—the *right* someone—would say, "Wow! Pastor Cook is certainly called of God!"

I found myself comparing my ministry to others and looking for my next big break, rather than seeking God to develop my character. I thought there were things I had to do—or not do—to make God like me more and give me the ministry to which I felt He had called me. This eventually produced jealousy in my heart. I was so afraid of failing that I felt like I needed to have a nod of approval from someone "important" to validate me as a pastor, and even more so as a man. I did not understand then how being rejected by my father when I was a child was still influencing my life.

Even though there were several factors involved in my downfall, and many of them out of my control, I could have made different choices. A good friend of mine said this once in a weekly message to his congregation, "Don't let people's criticism kill and don't live for their praise." I wanted to feel appreciated and approved of by people in ministry. I wanted the pat on the back from those to whom I had submitted myself. This was to my own detriment, to the point I felt like I was failing if I didn't have their public approval of me and of my ministry.

Furthermore, I was afraid. I was scared motionless at times of being a failure, and I was terrified of someone seeing how frail I truly was spiritually. I felt like I had to show everyone what we were doing in the hopes that God would bless us. Often, we ask God to bless what we are doing instead of asking

Him to lead us to do what He's blessing! Psalm 127:1 says, *"Except the Lord build the house, they labour in vain that build it..."* I worked hard, and I do believe I did so with every intention of building the church and building the Kingdom, but my priority in doing so was not correct. Fear and pride were weighing me down.

Reflection

In Luke 18:10-13, Jesus tells a story of two men who had come to the temple to pray—a Pharisee and a tax collector. Now, there weren't very many people in ancient Israel more despised than tax collectors, who were viewed as dishonest and deceitful. The Pharisee, though, was viewed as a respected and pious man.

When they came into the temple, the tax collector headed for the back, but the Pharisee went right to the front of the room. His prayer was full of self-promotion, and he spoke in a voice loud enough for everyone to hear. He thanked God that he was not like various sorts of evil men, or even like the tax collector, pointing his religious finger at the poor dude in the back. He wanted some sort of recognition.

When we pray, it is good to recount the things God has done for us. However, we have to guard our hearts against becoming prideful in our piety. We strive to be good. We strive to listen to His Word. We strive to do good works, so that men may see them and come to the saving knowledge of Christ. But we cannot think for a minute that any of this is our own doing. God will exalt whomever He wills, and if that's not us, or if it's not our time, then we must learn to accept it in humble obedience.

This Pharisee was wrong. So are many Christians and Christian leaders today. We set ourselves ablaze, so people can watch us burn. God is not nearly as concerned about our charisma and our giftings as He is with our character and our heart. *Somewhere in my life, I lost sight of this.*

I really believed in my calling and in the vision He gave me for my life and ministry. However, I thought it all had to move along at my pace. I set myself up to fail—and fail miserably. God's timing is not our timing.

Isaiah 40:31 says, *"But they that wait upon the Lord shall renew their strength; they shall mount up with wings as eagles; they shall run, and not be weary; and they shall walk, and not faint."* Here's the thing: if you have a vision or a calling from the Lord, you have to move out in it, there's no question about that.

However, in doing so, you must learn to wait for God's timing in the progress of the vision and the calling. You won't build it all overnight. If you wait patiently, while passionately pursuing the *face* of God and the *heart* of God, you will continually be renewed. That's what the prophet Isaiah was saying: if you want to mount up, or move upward as an eagle does toward the sun, then you must wait on the Lord. If He called us, He is responsible for the results, not us.

6

THE PINHOLE WIDENS

I have worked with high school students for several years as a school counselor and coach. I've had countless conversations with students over the years about many different problems. One thing has been consistent throughout these interactions: it seems as though the students—and many parents as well—wanted to focus on what everyone else was doing rather than owning their own actions and working to improve their own performance and behaviors.

We do not need to continually rehash the things that other people did to us. I could tell you a story about how others did me wrong. I could cry you a river over how badly we were treated. However, we really only have control over ourselves. We can control our effort, our attitude, and our response to others or to situations that arise in our path. What others do to us is not our concern.

In the first five years I served as a senior pastor, we had seven major church splits. I had every so-called prophet in the region show up at my church. We dealt with a spiritual stronghold of division and a spirit of Jezebel in our small city. When I talked with other pastors in the region, they told me they struggled with the same things with the same people who believed themselves to be prophets.

More often than not, it was a spiritual struggle to gain control of the church. Jezebel is first mentioned in the book of 1 Kings. She was the wife of King Ahab and wanted control more than anything else. She was a manipulative woman who sought to silence the voice of God in Israel.

I had one person after another show up at our church and try to take control and dominate the ministry during services, our day-to-day processes, our vision—literally every area of the church.

When our church grew, it grew because people came to us from other churches, not because souls were being saved. Something I failed to realize was that when the Jezebel spirit shows up, it's because you're making an impact on the devil's territory.

We did some very good things in that community while we were there. We were on the radio twice a week. One broadcast was geared toward teens and was on a contemporary Christian station in our area, and the other program was more traditional in its approach. We hosted a regional Christian television program about once a month, and we even had our own television program on the local cable access channel that aired weekly.

I had the opportunity to minister in Nigeria, and we had an amazing time there. One of our church members came with me to help me with capturing some of our meetings on video. I preached in churches of thousands and ministered in open-air crusades where we saw healings, miracles, and salvations every night. We were partnering with a ministry that drilled wells in villages without clean water to drink.

I went to Kenya twice, which was by far the greatest ministry experience I have had. I worked with a tremendous man of God there, one of the humblest servants of the Lord I've ever met. God moved in mighty ways in the churches and crusades in Kenya, with signs, wonders, miracles and salvations following. I really thought that this was going to be what God used to launch me forward in ministry.

Our church opened and ran a fully licensed day care center out of our building as well. My wife was the spearhead of this effort, as it was dear to her heart. We serviced some 50-70 children every day. This opened doors of opportunity for us to minister to families we would not have met otherwise, and we built some amazing relationships with those families, a few of which still exist today. My wife worked hard on this. She often worked without pay, just to make sure the program ran smoothly, and that our staff members were paid on time.

Despite all the wonderful things we were doing, we just could not gain any traction for the church in the community. I tried to form relationships with various people around town. I was even invited by one of the county judges to come lead a morning devotion and pray with him and his staff a couple of times each month. However, it seemed that no matter what we tried, we were cut off by people or things outside of our control. We experienced church split after church split, and it was taking a toll on me and my family in every conceivable way.

The last major church split came on a day when we had our largest number in attendance, several visitors, and even some unsaved people in the house. There was a man at the service who believed himself to be a prophet. He walked up to me and told me he needed the microphone after the song was over, because he had a prophetic word for the church. I asked him what it was, and he looked at me as if I had no right to ask. I said, "I'm the pastor, and I am responsible for this congregation."

He went on arguing with me in the middle of praise and worship because I would not give him permission to give a word to the congregation about how I had divided the church. When I walked up to the platform to try to regain control of the service, the worship leader came to my side and said, "It's hardly fair. You have a microphone, and he doesn't!" I told him to leave the platform and never come back. Over the next few minutes, the entire worship team walked out. We never recovered from that.

I was so rattled by the constant fight over that five-year span of time, I wasn't even able to pray. In my mind, I just could not understand how we could be doing so many wonderful things, yet we were still unable to get our ministry off the ground. There was a constant gnawing at my mind and spirit, wondering when my break and my exposure would come. I was so insecure—the desire for validation that I sought continued to gnaw at my heart.

Our church was declining, and I couldn't keep it going. I was working two jobs, and my wife and children were stressed constantly. We faced multiple situations financially where our light and water bills were behind. More than once, I came home to a house that was as dark as the night, with a notice on my door informing me that our electricity had been cut off. We couldn't do anything about it until first, we came up with the money to pay the bill, and second, until we could get in touch with someone to pay it. That created quite a lot of turmoil in our home.

We were giving, believing and hoping that God would come through, but we just never really saw any breakthrough in our ministry or at home. The stress of the constant struggle and the lack of resources put a strain on our marriage. We had times of intense disagreement in our home. There were even times when we didn't speak to each other for several days at a time.

While all this was going on at home, I was still trying to lead the ministry under my care. I would leave the house in the morning—sometimes before sunrise—and work at the church until around noon. Then, I would go to my second job and work until 9:30 at night. I was physically and mentally exhausted, and it showed most in my relationship with my wife and children.

In the spring of 2003, we merged our church with another church in the area. We planned to be there for two years, but that position only lasted eight months. It was supposed to be a period of restoration for us, while we worked to build the church in that region and prepared for what God had for us after that. At the time, I thought it was a strategic move which would provide a connection that would get me where I thought God wanted me to be. Over the first few weeks, we did some good things in that church. We worked out some challenges they had, and we began to stabilize in our situation as well. But in retrospect, this merger was not our best option.

Around July of 2003, we signed a lease on a rental house, so we could be closer to the church. Over the course of that summer, I began seeking God about what He would have us do next.

As I began to develop ideas for future ministry, I shared that with the pastor. Within a few days, we were released from employment at the church. We left that area right at Christmas-time in the same year we went there. We headed back home, greatly frustrated and discouraged.

I did not seek God's face; I sought His hand. I wanted Him to *do* something *for* me more than I wanted Him to *reveal* Himself *to* me and perfect what he had begun in me. Of course, I realize that perfection in life is not possible, but pursuit of excellence *is* possible and very necessary. However, I had all of this confused.

I thought I had to be like *this* preacher or *that* evangelist. I thought I was following God. I thought I had to follow what others were doing and do things like they were doing them—rather than seeking God for His plan for me. I knew all of this, but I just wasn't doing it. I was trying to keep my family afloat financially, while leading the church, and keeping up with the other ministry activities we had going on. I allowed my personal walk with Jesus to decline.

Pinholes Popping Everywhere

My life experiences prior to my time in ministry had a profound impact on how I approached life in general. Living in times of lack, watching my mother go through terrible depressions and near nervous breakdowns, and feeling isolated and alone were all a part of my makeup. I believed that, by the grace of

Chapter 6: The Pinhole Widens

God, I could work my way out of this. However, work apart from faith nets little in the grand scheme of God's eternal plan.

When we began facing failure in ministry, I immediately reverted to the litany I knew all too well:

"*It must be me.*" A pinhole opens.

"*I don't measure up.*" Another pinhole.

"*I'm not good enough to do this.*" Another pinhole.

"*No one will ever want to be associated with someone who wasn't acceptable to their own father.*" Yet another pinhole.

"*God's promises must apply to everyone except me and my family.*" Another pinhole, again. I felt like my wife and children were suffering because of me, and there was nothing I could do to help them.

For years, I believed that God was going to use my life experiences as part of what He called me to do. In fact, I still believe that. However, the challenges I faced as a child were never really addressed. I wanted so very badly to be accepted as a son. There were doors cracked open in my life that needed to be closed.

As a child, I compared my life to the lives of others around me. When I began facing failure in my adult life, I reverted to this same mentality. I became paralyzed with fear, thinking I'd end up just like my parents. I was afraid I would fail so miserably that I could never rebound from it. I just wanted to be like other people, at least the way I perceived them to be.

The people of Israel began comparing themselves to other nations around them. God's desire was to be the King of His people, but they couldn't see His hand in their life because of their own pride. In 1 Samuel 8:6, they cried out for a king, and God obliged them.

Throughout Israel's history, they had kings who were good and did right in the sight of God, but they also had many kings who did not follow the Lord. In fact, they became a divided nation, with the land of Judah splitting off from the rest of the nation. After a series of wake-up calls, they finally ended up in Roman bondage. It all began with the request to be like other nations and have a king. That is why the Bible says that comparing yourself to others is not wise (2 Corinthians 10:12): it will lead only to frustration and bondage.

Reflection

What about you? Have you tried to be like someone else? Have you tried to emulate someone else's business model? Have you tried to teach like another teacher in your school, because they have better scores in their classroom than you do in yours? Are you constantly trying to improve your resume for a better position, more money, and influential social circles? The examples could go on and on, but they really all reflect the same thing.

It is important to understand that we can and should learn from others, and we can and should take concepts learned from others and apply them to our life and to our work. But when we try to change the core of who we are, we have allowed ourselves to open the door to the gnawing of our enemy.

When I began to compare myself to other people, I began to measure my success based on what others were doing who were successful in my eyes. Success cannot be measured this way. Sure, there are certain things that our culture views as success, such as educational attainment, financial solvency, and family stability. It is not wrong to pursue these and other goals. What I wanted was to grow in ministry, but I really didn't understand what that actually meant.

When I began questioning God and comparing myself to others, I was moving very quickly toward condemning and judging others. It is not my job to condemn or judge others, nor is it their job to condemn or judge me. That is up to God. When we look at the things others are doing and expect the same thing to happen for us, we are missing the mark.

The scriptures say that God causes it to rain on the just and the unjust (Matthew 5:45). Therefore, we have to let it go. If we spent more time focusing on our own life and our relationship with the Lord, we wouldn't have time to worry about what others are or are not doing.

Everything in the Kingdom of God is contrary to popular culture. Jesus said that if any man wanted to follow Him, he must first deny himself, then take up his cross and follow Him (Luke 9:23). To deny yourself is to relinquish your own interests and focus on what interests God. Hebrews 12:1 instructs us to "...*lay aside every weight, and the sin which doth so easily beset us...*"

These small thoughts, these small sins, tend to take root in our lives and lead to larger problems down the road if we leave them unaddressed. We can get so wrapped up in our calling that we forget to be a Christian! Our vocation is not

Chapter 6: The Pinhole Widens

the sum total of who we are, but it is rather a means by which we can serve Him. To "*take up our cross*" is to be conformed daily to the image of Christ. We are a reflection of Him in the earth.

There can be no success apart from obedience. We must strive to be true to our calling, and we must be distinctive in our execution. We must do what God has designed us to do. Anything other than obedience to God, to His Word, to His commands, and to His direction for our lives is disobedience and is rooted in the gnawing sin of pride. Otherwise, we justify ourselves, rather than allowing Him to justify us. In doing so, we allow the devil to gain a foothold in our life. Once he's there, he won't leave easily.

I can't be something or someone that I was not created to be. I will not be the next Bill Gates, the next Sam Walton, the next Walt Disney, or the next Billy Graham. I can only be me. This is what is so amazing about God: He created each one of us in His image and in His likeness, yet we each have a unique and specific purpose in His plan.

You are not made to be anyone other than who you are. With all of your faults, and in spite of all of your failures, *you are the best you that ever existed*! What God wants is for you to develop your character and your integrity, so He can infuse you with the power to accomplish all He has called you to do.

When the palmerworm attacks, he will continue to gnaw at you until he opens a hole in your life. The gnawing sins of pride and fear will take root, unless we strive for authenticity: authentic love, authentic faith, and authentic relationships. You are an original, not a copy, so don't try to copy others. Learn from others, glean from others, receive from others, but be who God has designed *you* to be. He has a plan just for you! You can close the door on the attack of the palmerworm, and trust God to seal up the pinholes!

David Cook

7

LIVING IN THE FOG

In ancient times, war was not a long-distance affair. Your enemy was someone you could see and with whom you struggled face-to-face. The archers could attack from a short distance, but the foot soldier's only way to neutralize the enemy was to get within arm's reach of them. It was a dangerous—and sometimes costly—undertaking.

Joel 1:4 uses four terms to describe an attacking army, which he describes as being like locusts that are coming through the land. The palmerworm, or *gnawing* locust, represented the first wave of the attack. The gnawing locust made small, pinhole openings that if left unchecked, led to much more significant issues down the road.

The second level of attack mentioned in Joel 1:4 is the *swarming* locust. This term is used to describe the immensity of the attack arrayed against them. Some commentators speculate that the army was so large and so loud that it was nearly impossible to see or hear anything else. Can you picture the choking clouds of dust on the landscape stirred up by the pounding of the soldiers' feet? Can you imagine the ding of armor clanking and orders being shouted up and down the ranks of the army? The sky would have been darkened by the swarms of arrows released in battle. Isaiah 9:5 says, *"For every battle of the warrior is with confused noise, and garments rolled in blood."* The result of such conditions would have been disorientation, panic and fear.

The Fog of War

Combat veterans, when relating their experiences on the battlefield, often describe their struggle with the phenomenon called the "fog of war." This phenomenon is when the sounds, sights and effects of the battle create conditions that make it difficult to see, hear or know where the enemy is and where their brothers-in-arms are. Often, they report an almost deafening noise, which disorients them to the point that they cannot determine who is for them and who is against them.

When we get into a situation where failure is imminent, the fog in our minds gives place to the loss of vision. The thoughts that swarm and swirl around us cloud our ability to see our way clearly. We cannot hear anything but the buzzing of our past and the sound of panic trampling our mind. At this point, we have allowed pride and fear to grow in our hearts and minds to the extent that we cannot see past our problems. We hear people say, "Turn to God! He will help you!" And we wonder how we can turn to God when we can't see in any direction. Where is He?

When we lose our vision, we cannot move. We become stifled by fear, and we become directionless in our approach to God. As such, our relationship with Him deteriorates to the point that it is almost, if not entirely, non-existent. Sure, we may still go to church and try to act like everything is fine, but we have lost our way.

We look for enemies under every bush, behind every pulpit, and seated in every pew. Those who are supposed to be for us seem to be against us, and those who are against us seem to be for us. We cannot tell the difference because of our clouded view and our blocked vision. At this point, we might fire our weapon at anything that moves without regard for who or what we might strike.

There are no perfect churches. If you or I ever do find one, neither of us should go there because we will mess it up! There are no perfect churches because there are no perfect people. Think about it! The church is full of sinners saved by grace through faith in Jesus Christ. At church, we will find drug dealers, liars, thieves, adulterers, murderers, perverts, addicts, alcoholics, cheaters—and that's just the pastoral staff in some cases. We were all just a bunch of sinners who are saved by grace through faith in Christ Jesus.

Not everyone in the church is on the same pace in their relationship with God, and indeed, the devil has planted some intelligence gatherers in the church so that he can try to divide and destroy believers. They are like the forerunners to the army in Joel 1, enemy forces infiltrating the land—lying in wait, amassing intelligence, and waiting for their time to strike.

Loss of Vision

This story isn't everyone's story—and many people have faced things that are much worse—but this story is mine. When you fail, and God shows mercy to you, it leaves a deep impression on your heart. I can't begin to comprehend why He loves me, or why He chose to pursue me. We have all heard people say, "I found the Lord." I didn't find Him, that is for certain! I've heard it said this way, "You didn't find the Lord for two reasons: 1) He wasn't lost and 2) You wouldn't know where to look!" I certainly didn't know where to look, but He pursued me, apprehended me, and saved me!

Fast forward to our experience in St. Louis. I had very quickly, in just a matter of a few months, lost my vision and entered into my own form of the fog of war. After the eight-month stint in the church merger that was supposed to last two years, and the failed attempt at ministry before that, coupled with the strain and toll that situation had taken on our family in every possible way, we found ourselves homeless and nearly broke by January of 2004. I decided I had to leave the ministry.

For a period of time after we left Ohio, we ended up living in a hotel. One night while we were sitting down to eat our dinner out of a crockpot with our three children, I broke for the first time. I felt like everything collapsed on top of me. The noise of my failure was so thunderous that I couldn't think clearly. I could not see the vision I felt God had given me, and I most certainly could not hear His voice in my life. I was spiraling downward at a breakneck pace. I realized how foolish I had been, and it seemed like every mistake I had made over the past few years was flashing before my eyes.

Sometimes this sort of thing is generational. My parents had been married for ten years when they divorced. Up to that point, we had moved from house to house and never owned anything. What I can remember of my dad is that he would run off and leave us alone to do whatever it was he was doing. He would be gone for weeks, months or even up to a year at a time. He would make promises he never kept.

We struggled financially. Neither of my parents graduated from high school. I was an only child, so loneliness was typical for me, especially since we moved around so much when I was younger. I recall hearing my mother cry night after night. I remember the bruises on her face, and the lies she told me to cover for what was happening.

My mother felt like a complete and total failure as a parent, and I knew she did. She tried to overcompensate for it, as I was all she had in this life. We went through times of poverty where we had little to live on, and occasionally times that were not as bad. Eventually, we ended up living in a mobile home park, and even that mobile home was not hers. She always kept working, and she always kept me in school. She encouraged me to continue my education, but she was terrified that I would leave home and never return.

In many ways, I am thankful for the experiences I had as a child, or I may have never known how to get back up again after being beaten down. We currently live one mile from my mother. God has done such a beautiful work in her life! She made some decisions that affected my life, no doubt about it. But God is gracious, and I'm so thankful we live in the age of grace.

But many of the challenges I had faced in my life had gone unaddressed— the issues with my dad, the struggles my mother had when I was a child, our attempt at the ministry that seemed to have failed. I felt isolated and alone. Like the fog of war, the thoughts of my past created a loud and all-consuming voice of failure in my heart and mind. I couldn't see or hear any way out of it.

That night in January, right there in that hotel room on the southwest side of St. Louis, I got mad at myself and God. I took my ordination card out of my wallet and cut it into as many pieces as possible. I don't even know where I got the scissors to cut it up, but I know I did it.

I began saying aloud, "You can't do this. You can't take care of your family. You have no home, no job, no ministry. God didn't call you. You are a FAILURE! You are nothing but a loser. You don't have a degree or a career. All of your friends are college graduates, have homes, and are doing well. Look at you! If God called you, where are your followers? Where are your leaders? He has LEFT you! You are NOTHING, and you will never be anything more than that! You need to QUIT!"

Psalm 73:21-22 says, *"When I became embittered, and my innermost being was wounded, I was a fool and did not understand. I was an unthinking animal toward you"* (CSB). This is not a good place to be. This is bitterness toward God, and it will drive you far from Him. Bitterness stifles joy and peace, and it leads to separation from fellowship with God and with other believers.

I felt more alone at this point in my life than I had ever felt in the past. I thought I had nowhere to turn and no one to help me. My mind went back to that night in Columbus, Ohio, when I didn't know what I was going to do to provide for my family, or how I was going to clean up the financial mess I had due to the government shutdown. I believe God was trying to remind me of

Chapter 7: Living in the Fog

how he had worked in that extremity, but I refused to hear it. The stakes were so much higher this time.

Confusion swirled in my mind to the point that I couldn't see or hear from God at all. I couldn't even understand how God could love someone like me. My family history wasn't stellar; I came from nothing, so I just figured I'd always be nothing. I believed that I had no gifts or abilities that were of any benefit to anyone, and I just needed to find some mindless job to provide for my family. Even if there were nothing else, at least I had to do that. I completely let go of my hope in Christ. My wife tried to talk to me, but I couldn't hear her because of the resounding noise of failure in my head.

Isolation is an illusion, and it is the goal of the enemy. He cannot defeat us when we are united and in constant fellowship with Jesus and with other believers. It's when we break fellowship and are alone that Satan can do his work to destroy us. I had done just that. I had broken fellowship with people that I trusted and loved, and who were on my side. I couldn't believe that anyone would still be on my side, so I just broke off fellowship completely.

Fear led me to become protective and territorial. I considered anything that anyone said to me that touched the sore spot in my life offensive. Acting on that fear became my method of operation, and it spilled over into my marriage and my family for years after that. Like a soldier in the fog of war, I would strike out at whatever I didn't understand. I functioned in my home using fear as my leverage because I was afraid.

That night in the hotel room after I cut up my ministerial credentials, I said, "I WILL fix this." I concluded that it was my mess—which was actually a correct conclusion—and that I alone was responsible for fixing it. The problem with my thinking was that I refused to pray and ask God for mercy, for help, and for a way out. I just gave up on faith and decided that works were my answer.

While we were living there in the hotel, a great friend of ours helped us out financially, and we were finally able to move into an apartment. He organized a love offering from some people we knew when we were in Bible college (Thanks, Mark). Even when this was happening, I couldn't see that others were standing in solidarity with us before the Lord. I was so blinded by fear, by resentment, by shame, by guilt, by anger, by regret, and by my own words inside my head.

We found jobs and life started to level out a little bit. However, the damage to our lives was done, and it was immense. We went to church, we listened to the preacher, we asked for prayer, we lifted our hands, and we tried to appear to have it all together. However, we knew that things were going south, and they were going there fast. I knew that I was depleted spiritually.

A couple of months later, the pastor of the church we attended asked me to teach a Sunday School class. I reluctantly agreed to do so. I tried to do it with minimal prayer and little preparation. I tried to do it just from what I knew. After all, I had been a senior pastor, I had attended Bible college, and I had spent time studying the Scriptures. I thought I had this.

However, there was a gentleman in the class who started arguing with me one Sunday over semantics, and that was it. I wasn't going to do it anymore. People didn't care. I felt that God hadn't called me anyway, and I was tired of this sort of fighting.

The reality of it was that I would've done anything to silence the steady voice of failure in my ears. It was loud, it was blinding, and it kept me from peaceful rest. Four months after I came to this region with a desire to serve God, I completely and entirely quit the ministry. My pinhole opening had grown to a gaping floodgate. I had given place to the devil and allowed my life to be overcome by the swarming locusts of fear and defeat.

Reflection

In spite of all this, God never left me, and God has not left you. He hasn't moved or changed His mind about you. He still loves you, and He still has plans for your life. Nowhere in Scripture are we promised a life without struggle or pain. However, God's Word promises a life of victory. If there were no struggles, there could be no victories. If there were no illnesses, there could be no healing. If there were no devils, there could be no deliverance.

Revelation 12:11 says that we overcome by the blood of the Lamb and the word of our testimony. Our testimony is this: *our story*. We win by telling people how God saw us through. You may not be able to see Him, hear Him, or feel Him in your life right now, but rest assured, He is there. You are not alone.

The devil is a liar. You are the head and not the tail; you are above and not beneath. God has crushed Satan under Jesus' feet—the battle is already won.

Chapter 7: Living in the Fog

We win because of the work of restoration completed on Calvary. If you hear nothing but failure in your mind, and if you feel alone, know this: He will NEVER leave you nor forsake you. He promised to be with you always. You don't have to walk the road of regret, or the painful path your parents took, and you certainly do not have to face life's challenges alone. You can stop right now, ask God to rebuke the enemy on your behalf, and begin receiving your restoration from Him today!

David Cook

8

NOW THE FLOOD

It is amazing to me how someone with no physical sight can learn to navigate the world around them. It's incredible to me to see a person who has no eyesight walk through town, work at their job, live on their own, and function in our society. Imagine, if you will, what it must be like never to experience the light of day. Never to experience a sunrise or a sunset. Never to see the faces of your children. We use our vision every day to find our way through the world around us.

Proverbs 29:18 says, *"Where there is no vision [no redemptive revelation of God], the people perish; but he who keeps the law [of God, which includes that of man]—blessed (happy, fortunate, and enviable) is he"* (AMPCE).

When we lose our vision in Christ, we become spiritually blind. We have lost our faith, and we are groping through life without a clear understanding of our purpose in God.

In 2 Corinthians 5:7, Paul records these words, *"For we walk by faith (we regulate our lives and conduct ourselves by our conviction or belief respecting man's relationship to God and divine things, with trust and holy fervor; thus we walk) not by sight or appearance"* (AMPCE).

Vision illuminates the avenue of faith, so we can follow Christ in all areas of our lives. Where there is no vision, it is difficult, if not impossible, to walk by faith. Where there is no faith, fear takes over. When we are operating from a position of fear, we believe *we* can control the results, which is synonymous with pride—and pride is where sin begins. Following Christ requires faith, and we must seek Him daily to grow in it. As we do, He reveals His vision to us and shows us how to walk out His plan for our lives.

The Spiritual Swamplands

I live near the Mississippi River. There are a number of smaller creeks and streams that run into the Mississippi in our area. The banks of these waterways provide structure, guidance, and direction to the water. As long as the water stays within its banks, it flows with power, and it flows in a clearly defined direction.

Vision creates riverbanks in our lives. Jesus said that out of our belly would flow *"rivers of living water"* (John 7:38). Rivers need banks to flow, and you and I need vision to survive.

When the Bible says that people will perish without vision, it means they will have no restraint and run wild, like a river without banks—which is nothing but a swamp.

When the Mississippi River floods, the smaller creeks and streams around us will flood as well. When the river overflows its banks, destruction follows. Swamps have no banks, and they are full of snakes, alligators, and insects. The water is murky, and you cannot see under the surface. Floods are dangerous, and I have seen firsthand the trail of destruction left behind. One might say that a flood is the result of a river flowing without the restraint of banks, running wild wherever it desires.

Another thing to consider about floods is that water will always flow toward a low spot. During a flood, destruction is more intense to those homes and businesses in the low-lying areas. The same is true when we are without vision in our life. We end up living in low places spiritually. We have no direction, and our vision is gone. The destructive forces of the enemy will find us at our lowest point and will try to utterly overwhelm and destroy us.

Isaiah 59:19 begins, *"When the enemy shall come in like a flood...."* Satan will seek out the low areas of our lives and try to flood them. If we are weak in our finances, he will attack there. If we are weak in the realm of sexual purity, he will attack there. If we are weak in faith, he will attack with doubt. If we're weak in the field of confidence and hope, he will attack us with fear and unbelief. The enemy only needs a small opening to begin, and if we give him that opening, he will bombard it!

The second part of that verse in the Amplified Bible says, *"... the Spirit of the Lord will lift up a standard against him and put him to flight [for He will come like a rushing stream which the breath of the Lord drives]"(AMPCE)*. Here, the Scripture says God moves like a *"rushing stream,"* or a river with banks. He's a God of order.

In Genesis 9, the Bible records a story of something that happened to Noah following the flood. Noah began planting vineyards, and he made some wine from the fruit. Noah drank the wine and became drunk from it. His son Ham found him uncovered in his tent.

There are varying interpretations of what occurred next. We don't know what actually happened, but suffice it to say that whatever it was, it was bad enough for Noah to later curse his own son.

We can see here a tactic of the enemy. He will take advantage of us at our lowest point. When we can't see, hear or feel God, the enemy will try to flood us when we are the most vulnerable. When Noah's other sons, Shem and Japheth, found out about their father's condition, they took a garment and covered him up.

I always wondered why Shem and Japheth walked in backward to cover Noah. I believe the application for us is that this is a type of what happens to us in repentance. The boys came in with their backs toward Noah, refusing to look at their father's sin or to take advantage of his vulnerability. They covered him, not allowing anyone else to see him exposed and weak.

When the blood of Jesus is applied to our lives, we are covered by His strength and His grace. Hebrews 13:8 states that Jesus is the same yesterday, today, and forever (paraphrased). He covers my past, He preserves my present, and He secures my future! When I get to where I'm going, He will be there. God is always moving us forward and chooses to forget our sins when we repent of them. Without a doubt, He will use other people to help us and cover us when we are weak.

The devil wants to capitalize on our low spots and flood them like a swamp with disorder and destruction. Our low-lying areas are susceptible to attack, no question about that. However, if we stay in fellowship with God and with other believers, we will have protection. We don't have to allow ourselves to be swept under by the filthy floodwaters of the adversary.

We can call on the Lord, and He will protect us; we can call on our brothers and sisters in the Lord and ask them to cover us in prayer. Then, the marshy areas will be filled with God's presence, with divine healing, and with magnificent peace—giving NO PLACE to the devil!

In my time of crisis, I decided to break fellowship—so I was left uncovered. I didn't trust anyone with my struggle, and I felt that I could fix it on my own. I allowed a wedge to develop in my relationship with my wife, with my children, with my friends, and with my pastors. I broke fellowship and decided that I would just fix things myself, apart from God and others.

Without vision, you have no idea where to go or how to get there. You make life decisions by taking your best guess. One night when I was a child, I got out of bed and headed toward the bathroom. I was hurrying down the hallway and thought I had reached the point where the hall turned left. To my surprise, I crashed into the wall instead, and stubbed my left pinky toe on the edge of the wall. This was the second time that week that I had done the very same thing to the very same toe.

I can tell you that I had probably never thought much about my left pinky toe until that happened. But, at the moment of impact, every fiber of my being was instantly aware of that toe's existence and its current state of pain! My toe is still somewhat deformed from that experience, which serves as a reminder of how hard it is to grope around in the dark.

Spiritually, we do the same thing. We try to move with no light, with no revelation from God. We grope around when we have no vision. We can't hear, we are disoriented, and we are lost. We end up bumping into things and doing more damage than good. The destruction that is taking place may seem so immense that we cannot see past the pain.

Floating in Flood Water

In 1993, there was an unprecedented flood in the St. Louis region. My wife and I were engaged at the time, and I was on active duty in the United States Marine Corps stationed in Okinawa, Japan. My fellow Marines and I used to watch the news while we were working, getting a little taste of life back home.

One night, the Marine who was working with me said, "Hey Cook, come here. Your hometown is on the news!" As I came in, I saw a woman in a wedding gown riding in a bass boat, pulling up to the steps of a large Baptist Church in town. When they asked her what she was doing, she said, "The flood is not going to steal my wedding day! I'll get married even if I have to float to the church on the flood water!"

That bride showed such tenacity in realizing her dream that day. She was determined to get married, and nothing was going to stand in her way. However, floods are dangerous. While you may be able to navigate the streets by floating on the flood water, you can't see what is beneath the surface. Water levels can rise and fall at any moment.

Chapter 8: Now the Flood

By the spring of 2004, I had reached a point in my life in just a few short months where I had no relationship with Christ. My faith was gone, and I was rationalizing things in my mind rather than judging my life through the lens of scripture. I decided at that point to do it all in my own strength. I decided to go back to school and get a degree in business, and the process was going to take a while.

I was going to find success, and I didn't care about vision or calling or anything that had to do with my previous life in ministry. I even removed it from my resume. By April of 2004, I had completely cut myself off from everyone I knew while in the ministry, except for two people.

I was living with my wife and our three children in a small apartment, and I felt like it was up to me to fix this mess that I had created. I bought into the lie of the enemy that told me I could exalt myself, apart from the grace and favor of God.

I had gone back to school to find approval. I didn't have a degree when I moved in 2003. I was embarrassed by the fact that everyone I knew before I left to start my life had already been in their careers for some time. My upbringing was unconventional, and I wanted so badly to be "normal." I found myself far from it, so I forced it.

I had very minimal student loan debt when I moved back to Missouri. My Bible College education had been paid for in its entirety by the man I met in North Carolina, and I earned that diploma debt free. When I went back to school to earn my bachelor's degree, and later my master's degree, I was forced to take on a lot of debt.

Debt merely is our attempt to appear "blessed" when, in reality, we are just us putting ourselves into financial bondage. The Bible says that the borrower is the servant to the lender (Proverbs 22:7). I had put myself and my family into debt and bondage, and I had no real means to recover from it.

We began to rebuild our lives in a very different direction from ministry. I thought I'd have a great career with the company where I worked. Within my first two years, I had been promoted twice.

My company sent me to different facilities within the corporation to work with them as an advisor and address various needs and concerns related to my position. I was well-liked and respected, and I became an expert in my role there. I worked hard to grow in that job and to grow the position. Eventually, I sank into the lull of success and erased as much of my ministry life as possible. I even contacted the organization that had ordained me and told them to remove me from their mailing list, leave me alone, and never contact me again. I said I didn't need them, and I have made my way to take care of my family. Bitterness had taken root in my heart.

In the midst of what seemed to be a prosperous time for us, we still struggled. I thought we were starting to float, but we were floating in dangerous waters. We moved from an apartment to a house. We did a lease on the home, with the intent to purchase the property within two years. That fell through. During the move to Missouri, our credit had been ruined, and no bank would lend us the money to buy the home. We lost all the money we had paid into the house. Financial pressure is tough on a marriage, and we felt the effects of that pressure in our home.

We moved again in 2006 to be closer to our family. The family could help us out with our children, and I was hoping for a job to open up with the Federal Government. We were considering a move to Washington D.C. at that time, but I would have had to go about six months ahead of the rest of the family. I had two excellent opportunities, and neither one of them worked out. I eventually went to another company for a pay increase and less responsibility—seemed like a win, right?

In the midst of all of this, flood waters rose and fell in our lives, and financial pressure continued to mount. We came close to bankruptcy twice but managed to beat that wolf away from our door. As the economic pressures mounted, along with the uncertainty of what would happen with me professionally, it took a toll on our home. I started working later and sometimes just staying out late at night.

My wife and I didn't do anything together—we merely coexisted in the same house. The kids began to grow apart, and I felt like I was losing my relationship with them. And I was making things worse by propagating fear in my entire household.

We were finally able to buy our own home in 2008, and I was taking graduate classes to obtain my Master's Degree in Education. I made the career move in 2010 to go into the education field to finish the degree. I assumed a position where I was coaching two sports at the high school level. I thought I was finally where I belonged, and I enjoyed my work. I was able to have an impact on young people and felt I could possibly be a witness in a dark place—if the Lord would even use a man like me. (Anyone who works in public education understands just how dark a school can be, spiritually speaking.) Somewhere deep in my heart, I still had a desire to fulfill God's calling in my life.

The first couple of years of this were good. I was promoted to become the head coach of two varsity sports and felt that I had arrived at the place God had for me. I was trying to be a good person, but had let go of any possibility of what God had for me.

We began attending a remarkable church in 2008 in our hometown. However, I never spoke to anyone. I hid at church, and I hid the fact that I had a past in ministry. I preferred that no one ever know anything about me. I taught my athletes things like integrity, the value of hard work, humility and character. It all sounded good, and my reputation had grown in the community. For the first five years I was at the school, I thought I was finally home, vocationally speaking.

I knew I was having an impact on young people, but I also knew I was not right with the Lord. I had allowed sin to enter my life through a pinhole opening that had not yet been addressed. I was trying to serve Him in my own strength and made an absolute mess of everything I touched. My needs had become so huge, that I couldn't see any way to ever be out of debt and to stabilize my marriage and my home. The damage done in our lives was severe from an emotional perspective.

Never let anyone discount your fight. Emotional wounds are deep, and those who suffer them require a lot of grace to be healed and restored. I thought I was beginning to stand on solid ground, but what was beneath me was, in truth, very unstable. What I was rooting my life in was not sustainable.

Reflection

Often, when we lose our vision, we focus on something completely different. We think that we are doing the work of the Lord and may even have ourselves convinced we are living in complete obedience to Him. We may feel like we are standing firm, but we are floating on flood water, and that is unstable at best. Just because the initial rains are over, we can't get excited believing we are out of it all together. It's only a matter of time before the next wave will hit our lives.

God is not worried about how He is going to meet our needs. He has a plan, and He has the resources. He sent His Son to earth to die for our sins and to restore us to fellowship with Him. One word from heaven is the answer for us. It's all found in Jesus. I lost my vision, but God never did. I gave up, but God never did. I lied to myself, but God knew the truth. His word is everlasting, and it never fails! He will not let one word fall to the ground, and He will fulfill His promises.

The last part of Proverbs 29:18 says that the man who keeps the law—or operates in faith, following the vision of God—"*happy is he*." In other words, this man stands above the destruction of the flood waters. He is "*happy, fortunate and enviable*." He is happy, because the joy of the Lord is his strength. He is fortunate, because he has learned that he can rise above the battle, knowing the fight is not his, but the Lord's. He is enviable, because the favor of God encompasses him like a shield. This man stands above the flood waters, restored to fellowship with his Creator!

9

LICKING UP EVERY SCRAP

Joel mentions two final stages of locusts that came on the land. These final two attacks could almost be simultaneous due to what we know about the development of the insect. However, they were distinct in the level and type of destruction they brought about. One licked up the scraps of what was left after the first two waves of locusts passed through the land. The final locust, the devouring locust, consumed anything and everything that was left. To me, these final two waves are a picture of the lowest place of descent in my life.

Here is a brief look back at the order of destruction of the locusts:

- Palmerworm – Gnawing Locust
- Locust – Swarming Locust
- Cankerworm – Licking Locust
- Caterpillar – Consuming Locust

The cankerworm, or licking locust, ate up all the scraps, the bits and pieces left behind by those that went before him. The cankerworm had a firm grip and could sit for long periods of time-consuming fruit and green leaves.

The cankerworm refers to three areas of damage in our lives. First, the cankerworm may refer to the damage done by our own mouths. James 3:8 tells us that the tongue is difficult if not impossible to tame. I am confident this is why it is important for Christians to pray without ceasing (1 Thessalonians 5:17). If you consider the gifts of the Spirit, five of them involve speaking: word of prophecy, word of wisdom, word of knowledge, tongues and interpretation of tongues (1 Corinthians 12:8-10). Given that we may condemn our own lives and soul with the words of our mouth, it is imperative that we discipline our tongue.

Second, the cankerworm may refer to damage done by others as well. Gossip, slander, and lies all can cause unrepairable damage—even when these stories are based in truth or on our own actions.

Third, the cankerworm may refer to damage done by sin that has gained a significant foothold in our lives. Once we give place to the devil, he won't leave us easily. There's an old saying that says, "Old habits are hard to break." The cankerworm has a significant grip, and it can choke us at times. This brings to mind things like addictions, debt, habitual secret sins, and thought patterns. All of these things can stifle our growth and our ability to break free.

A Culture of Fear and Failure

As my wife and I were living the typical American life some ten years removed from ministry, the last two waves of the enemy's attack overwhelmed us. They issued a harsh blow to our home, our finances, and our marriage. I came to the realization very quickly as these last couple of waves hit our family that I was not standing firm on anything. The ground beneath my feet was very loose, and I felt as if I could lose it all at any moment.

Shortly after we moved into our own house, I fell to pieces. My wife and I were not communicating at all. We went to church, we worked our jobs, and did whatever we wanted in between—especially me. I was looking for a good time, and I felt I had found better friends in low places than I ever had in the church. We had begun drinking socially and found friends who had a form of godliness. They were good people. They worked hard. They paid their bills and their taxes, so it all seemed right to me.

About a month after we moved into our home, my wife and I had a blowup, and I thought we'd never recover from it. We had been married for 15 years and had three children, and I thought I was about to lose my family just like my father did. Although I worked and took care of my family, I felt I was no better than my dad who never took care of me and even disowned me. Now I was about to lose my family. This crisis was not the first crisis we had like this. However, this time, it seemed to be so final, so deep, and so intense. I knew that God was not in our midst to guide us through.

Over the course of the next several months, we managed to pull it together enough to go on, although things grew more and more difficult over the next three years.

One day, about two years after I took the job at the school in our community, I came home and got to the mailbox before my wife did. As I looked through the mail, I found one late bill after another. We were 90 days late on our mortgage, our car payment, our utilities, our insurance—everything. We were giving, but we weren't tithing.

I couldn't see any way that we could recover from this. I felt like the mistrust and the lack of communication had stifled our relationship. The blindness and confusion that we were living in kept us from sharing the most important things about our lives together. We were about 30 days from losing everything we had.

When my wife came home that evening, I was so angry and upset that I exploded on her. There was a lot of yelling and screaming. I recall being so mad, that I didn't know where our children were. They must have been home, but I can't remember. It was like I blacked out, I was so mad. I knew that I had created the culture of fear in our home, which was why she had been so afraid to tell me the ends had been a long way from meeting for several months.

In 2013, we ended up filing bankruptcy and went into a five-year repayment program. We were able to save our home, but the damage to our life, to our credit, and to our marriage and family was profound. I thought the licking locust had done all he could do, but I was wrong.

Over the next four years, we had major car problems almost monthly. We ended up losing a vehicle completely when the engine blew up. Under the bankruptcy, I couldn't obtain credit for a new car without court approval. Therefore, we had to take a small inheritance my wife received from her grandmother and use it to purchase a used car to get by. Thank God, He saw us through. Eventually, I had to ask the court for approval to incur debt to buy another vehicle so that we could have more reliable transportation. It seemed like anything that could break, did break on our vehicles and in our house, and I couldn't spend money to fix it.

Under the bankruptcy plan, I was required to account for all my income. Any inheritances, tax refunds, or other such monies we received had to be turned over to the court, or we had to prove we needed it. We really couldn't have savings to speak of, so all our repairs had to be paid in cash. It seemed like every single month, we had a significant expense. I tried to resume tithing but found it difficult. By the fall of 2014, I was utterly broke financially, entirely depleted spiritually, and barely there emotionally. I couldn't win at anything in life that mattered.

When God directs you, He is responsible for providing for you. When you take it all on yourself, then you are saying you do not trust Him to provide a way for you. In my attempts to appear blessed and to find some normalcy and approval from others, I incurred debt. Some debt isn't necessarily bad, but debt that cannot be adequately managed or repaid is nothing but bondage. I had tried my level best to make it appear that I had it together, but I didn't. I had allowed everything in my life to spiral out of control; I had no way to recover from it.

As if the bankruptcy weren't enough, we began sleeping in separate rooms. We didn't talk in any way other than by an email or text, because I didn't want to have any face-to-face conversations with my wife at all. I tried to craft my words carefully, hoping to avoid any fights. We had fought quite a bit over the past ten years, and I wanted to fix this financial mess. In all sincerity, I was afraid to talk to her. I was afraid to be open and honest. I was afraid to hear what she had to say. There were other periods of time when we slept in separate rooms of the house, but I believed our marriage was beyond help at this point.

At the time we filed the bankruptcy, I thought that all I had was now consumed and touched by the enemy. I had given him a place, and he took it all. I failed to realize that I still had breath in my body and life in my bones. I still had a place to sleep, and I still had a family, regardless of how dysfunctional I had made it. I gave place to the adversary, there is no doubt about that. He touched all that he could, but God is bigger and stronger than anything we could ever muster. Certainly, He is more powerful than any devil that might attack our lives.

I Hurt, So I Have to Hurt

The Bible is full of accounts of people who endured great hardships and overcame their challenges through the grace and mercy of the Lord. Job was one such man. God had such confidence in Job that he allowed Satan to attack him. Satan believed he could make Job curse God. The Bible records the account of how Job was afflicted with boils on his skin. He was so miserable he found himself sitting on an ash heap, scraping his skin with broken pottery.

I believe Job was cutting. Cutting has become a common method for people to deal with such things as depression. Most cutters only cut superficially, but there are some who cut much more deeply. Job was a cutter. Job was so far down in the dumps that he felt like he had to hurt more than he already was. He felt like he was so worthless that his body deserved punishment as an expression of the pain on the inside.

When we were living in the hotel in 2004, I refused to sleep in the bed. I felt like I didn't deserve it. Throughout the next ten years, regardless of who was at fault in any of the circumstances in my marriage and home, I felt that I bore the brunt of the responsibility and therefore deserved punishment. It might mean I slept on the couch, or didn't get to eat, or some other form of self-punishment. Sometimes we feel that we have no other way to express the pain in our own life but to hurt more. I am hurting; therefore, I must hurt more.

Job was hit hard and fast, but this wasn't the end of it. It got worse—much worse. While Job was processing one bad report, he got another. While he was processing that one, he got another. It was perpetual. His entire life's work suffered attack, and he lost nearly everything he had. His wife told him to curse God so that God would kill him and end his suffering. Job's friends came in with all kinds of advice. There will always be people who have an idea of what you should do to get out of your situation. Many of them mean well. But until you hear from God, you will never progress past where you are.

Job would not curse God. He questioned God, but he never cursed God. At the end of the book, the restoration that came to Job's life is a picture of our restored relationship to Christ through salvation. The blessing that occurred in the latter part of Job's life was greater than the blessing he lived under before.

Like the locusts, the enemy will try to devour and lick up all that you have. He will take your joy, your peace, your wealth, your health, your money, your relationships—all to get you to curse God.

No matter how bad it got in my life, I refused to ignore the fact that God was still God. I just thought He wasn't involved in my life anymore. I struggled to believe that He was concerned about anything that concerned me. I could see God moving for others, but I felt like I was never going to see any breakthrough myself. Thanks be to God, though, He never left me!

Malachi 3:11 tells us if we obey God in our giving, He will rebuke the devourer on our behalf. The devourer eats up and licks up everything in his path. In the Amplified Classic version, the word *devourer* is explained as insects and plagues. The passage goes on to say that these insects and plagues would no longer destroy our land—if we would live our life in obedience to God's plan and purpose. For God to rebuke the devourer, it meant there must have been one present, or one coming that the people could not yet see.

Reflection

In the book of Genesis, we see the story of creation. It's such an awesome thing to consider, how our God spoke this world into existence! He created man in His image, meaning we have His nature and His DNA in our being! If God's Words have creative power, and we are created in His image, then our lives are framed by our words. We can shape our future for the better or for worse.

Not only can our words shape our lives, they can affect other people as well. The words we say about our children, our spouse, our co-workers or classmates all have power to heal or hurt. My grandmother used to say, as did many others I'm sure, "If you can't say anything nice, don't say anything at all." Proverbs 18:21 tells us, *"Death and life are in the power of the tongue, and those who love it will eat its fruits"* (ESV).

Negative confessions will create an atmosphere that makes it nearly impossible for you to break out of the grip of sin. We must guard our mouths, and guard our responses to others, lest we find ourselves bound in the chains of depression, of sin, of debt, and of broken relationships. But thanks be to God, if His Word can create something from nothing, His Word can deliver me from the snare of the enemy!

10

DEVASTATED AND DEVOURED

I have a few odd habits related to food. First, I have a method of eating peanut M&M's. I sort them by color, and I only eat like colors together. In the event that I get an odd number of a given color, I will match off colors, but only certain ones. I will eat red and green together, because those are the primary colors of Christmas—and I like Christmas. I will eat blue and orange together because I am a Chicago Bears fan and those are the team colors of the Bears. I always eat red and green or blue and orange combinations last, because they're my favorites.

My point is that it takes me a bit longer to eat the M&M's that way, but I get it done in a methodical way. Joel 1:4 describes a methodical attack of enemy armies that came in four major waves. The first couple of waves came fairly quickly. They did their damage and moved on. But the last two were a bit slower, but lingering.

The final stage of the wave listed in Joel 1:4 is the caterpillar. This insect is the one that devours all. If there's anything left, this one takes it. The caterpillar may move a little slower than the other insects in this passage, but his damage is all-inclusive. He leaves no leaf untouched. If there's anything at all remaining, he will devour it.

One night, after my wife and I had exchanged several heated messages through email (because we wouldn't, and at times couldn't, talk without yelling and fighting) I was lying in bed after poring over our finances. We had just met with the attorney and paid our initial retainer fee to file bankruptcy. I told my wife, "You WILL help me pay this off, and then you can do whatever you want. I know that you will NEVER ruin me financially again. I'm going to sell this house, and you can go wherever you want to go. I don't need much, and I can't live this way."

My heart hurt so badly that day. I thought about what I had said to this woman, this mother, this wife. She had left everyone and everything to be with me. We had fought through some heavy stuff together. I pondered what my life would be like without her. After all, we had been married for twenty years at this point. She had barely turned 20 years old when we got married, and I had just turned 21. Life with her was all that I had ever known, and the same was true for her. In many ways, I just could not imagine life without her.

I lay in bed that night asking myself, "Is this it? Am I really going to end up divorced? What will that life be like?" I wept and cried as I considered a lonely life without my wife and children. I envisioned them all leaving me and going on to be happy. That same evening, I had a dream that I died in a hospital bed alone, and I was buried with no family around at all. In that dream, I saw myself becoming what I feared the most: a man just like my father.

Several days later, I asked Becca if we could talk after the kids went to bed. We sat down, fearful of where this conversation might lead. Our relationship was severely broken. I had no idea what I needed to do to fix it, but I knew that I had to try something. We had a long conversation, but it didn't net much. Discussions like this were something that cycled and repeated over the course of about two years from 2013 to 2015. We would talk, then we would fight and feel like it was over. Then we'd try to speak again, end up fighting, and so on.

I was so bitter and afraid that I refused to heal. My wife and I were finally forced to do more than talk—we had to communicate. We set ourselves to work things out in our marriage. I took over our financial management, and I decided this would NEVER happen to us again.

On the surface, life was improving after we filed bankruptcy. The football team I coached won a conference championship. Two years later they won two playoff football games for the first time in a long time in our school. Our track kids brought back a district championship and have repeatedly brought back either a 1st or 2nd place district trophy since I've been the head coach. Our girls' team even finished 2nd at the state meet in 2013, the same year I had to file for bankruptcy. It all seemed like it was good, but it wasn't.

I took over a technical education program at our school, serving as the coordinator for our students who were attending these courses at our community college. I grew the program from 17 students to over 60 students within the first three years that I was in charge. I gained the respect of my superiors as well as my peers in this new job. It seemed like I had found a place I could stay until I was ready to go, or until I was prepared to retire. But there were still some things in my life that were wrong. There were things I had

Chapter 10: Devastated and Devoured

allowed to take root in my heart that just needed to go.

In the middle of what seemed to be a rebound, my marriage was still suffering. Only a select few people knew anything of the bankruptcy or the troubles we were having in our marriage. We kept cycling through the same thing. We would try to talk, then something would come up, and I'd get mad and sleep in the basement for several days or weeks.

Additionally, my son and I had no relationship at all. He graduated from high school in 2013 and tried to join the military. He ran into some problems with his legs and was unable to complete the process, and for the next couple of years, he struggled to find his way. I was a horrible example of what to do when things go wrong. I was not there for him at the time he needed me most.

The following spring, my middle daughter and I had an argument that had been building for a while. We didn't speak for several months after this. She graduated from high school in 2014, and on the most important night of her young life, I didn't say a word to her. As I look back at that time, it seemed that everything in my life was coming unglued, and that I was losing everyone and everything that was important to me.

Our youngest daughter was always quiet and seemed to ignore some of this. She would smile and laugh, and at times, go to her room or basement to avoid listening to any of the turmoil in our home. I always felt like I had a good relationship with her, but I never really understood how it all affected her.

My wife is an excellent mom. Like most moms, she's protective of her children. I always felt like she was taking sides by trying to protect them when we would have problems with them. In retrospect, she wasn't taking sides at all. She was doing what I should have been doing as well: guiding them instead of driving them.

I drove them to work hard so that they wouldn't have to struggle like I did. The message was skewed, though. They felt like all I was worried about was me and how they made me look. To a certain extent, that was a correct assessment. As a staff member of the school, I wanted them to succeed and do well. I wanted them to excel beyond their peers. In some ways, I wanted recognition as a parent for their efforts. I can't say that I ever told them that directly, but I know they felt that way.

Completely Cut Off

Joel goes on to explain more about the destruction of the land of Judah. In Joel 1:7 he says, "*It has laid waste My vine [symbol of God's people] and barked and broken My fig tree...*" (AMPCE). Jesus referred to Himself as the vine in John 15 which says, "*...you are the branches. Whoever lives in Me and I in him bears much (abundant) fruit. However, apart from Me [cut off from vital union with Me], you can do nothing*" (John 15:5, AMPCE). I believed I had been cut from the vine, by my own doing.

After the bankruptcy, I realized that we had been devoured financially, emotionally, relationally, spiritually—in just about every way we could be. In Joel 1, the prophet goes on to describe the real destruction that came about on the land. In verses 10-11, he describes the nation as desolate and without fruit. Even the grapes that produced the sweet wine were all gone. Throughout scripture, wine is a symbolic description of the Holy Spirit. I couldn't sense the presence of God in my present situation at that time. It felt like the Holy Spirit was far from me.

Joel also says that all the oil was gone. Oil was used in the Old Testament to anoint God's leaders. It was also used as a description of the anointing of the Holy Spirit. While serving in ministry, I had prayed for people to be saved, healed, blessed, and delivered and had seen things happen right before my eyes! I had witnessed the healing of a woman in Kenya with an issue of blood. It dried up the moment we prayed, and she is whole to this day. All of that happened because of the anointing of the Holy Spirit, but yet now I couldn't even muster enough faith to talk to my wife and children or believe that God could heal our home.

Unsuccessfully Seeking Success

Joel goes on to say that those who work the land should be ashamed because the harvest in the field has perished. I was so ashamed of what my life had become. I wore a mask of confidence every day of my life. I tried to hide behind what little success I was experiencing, thinking that I could pull off the "fake it 'til you make it" trick.

Success is a tricky thing. In my first year as a head football coach, we had a great group of kids and coaches. We had such high hopes for that season, and everyone seemed to be excited about the prospects of a championship year at some level. We rolled out to our first game, and the opposing team played us tough and forced an overtime period. Our opponent had the ball first, and they scored by kicking a field goal. We had the ball last, and our running back dove into the end zone for a touchdown, which would have won the game. However, the ball came out of his grip at some point either right before or right after he hit the ground. Of course, I will argue to this day that it was a touchdown, but I was not the guy in the stripes who got to make the call, so we lost the season opener.

After that game, I was discouraged. Our team had experienced a great off-season preparing. Our staff worked so hard to get them ready to play not just for that game, but for the entire season. We had some excellent football players who wanted to compete and win. I was discouraged, wondering what I could have done differently.

On my staff that year was a long-time volunteer coach whom I've known for most of my life. He came up to me and put his hand on my shoulder and said, "Losing is terrible. I hate to lose more than I like to win, and I know you do, too. BUT there are about a billion people in China who could care less whether you won tonight or not, and the sun will come up in the morning. So, keep it in perspective."

I had become so consumed with shame. Shame is tied to what we think other people think about us. It's all about the image and the perception we believe that others have of us. Other people are not thinking about us as much as we *think* they are thinking about us. That may sound a bit odd, but really, we all have our own issues to battle. We could relieve ourselves of so much pressure if we stopped worrying so much about what we *think* other people think of us.

The Strength of Joy

In Joel 1:12, the prophet describes how the invaders destroyed the palm tree that offered shade. There were no apples, pomegranates, figs—nothing! Nothing was exempt from destruction. As such, even the "…*joy has withered and fled away from the sons of men*" (Joel 1:12, AMPCE). As you read on, you will see that food was cut off, joy and gladness were gone from the house of God, the seed was rotten, and the barns were in ruin. Even the beasts and animals were struggling. An all-consuming fire had laid to waste the land that had once been so alive.

When we allow the gnawing to take hold, and our vision becomes blocked, we cannot see or hear what God has for us. That gives place to the devourer. It may look good on the cover, and we may sound good and say all the right things. We can speak from our heads, from what we learned or read or heard someone else say. We can "name it and claim it" or "blab it and grab it" all we want! The anointing is gone. The joy of our salvation is gone. We are cut off, or so it seems, from the grace of God.

We ran a daycare center in our ministry when we pastored in Ohio. We had one young boy who was quite disrespectful to his mother. At one point, she asked me for advice on how to deal with him. I told the lady, "The problem with your son isn't what he does or says today. The problem is that it was allowed to start."

Although external factors beyond my control enhanced the struggles I faced in my life, the fact remains that I allowed them to happen. Those things that were out of my control simply magnified what was already happening in my life. The devourer came in, and he devoured! He ate up all my increase and nearly destroyed my family in the process. As the priest of my home, I had very few options. I became ashamed, as were those workmen in Joel 1:12. So I hid in shame.

I failed my wife. I failed my children. I failed my pastor. I failed my friends. I failed financially. I failed in ministry. I failed as a man, and I failed God. In my mind, I was no better than my parents and was now facing a rapid race to the bottom of the pit of life.

Reflection

Satan has no power over you, except for what you allow him to have. That is why it is SO important for you to understand his devices, so that you can resist him when he attacks. If you resist, he WILL flee! But resistance apart from a relationship with Christ is powerless. In Acts 19, some men tried to cast out devils in the name of "...*Jesus whom Paul preacheth*" (v. 13). The devils responded to them and said, "...*Jesus I know, and Paul I know; but who are ye?*" (v. 15). You can't just decide to take a stand without first having a thriving relationship with Jesus.

In John 11, Jesus came to the tomb of His friend Lazarus. Lazarus had been dead now for four days and had been buried in a tomb. After He called Lazarus forth, Jesus noticed that the grave clothes still bound Lazarus. Several years ago, while ministering in Nigeria, the Lord spoke to me about this and said, "There are many people who believe in me but are still bound by their sin—like grave clothes." Jesus said in John 11:44 concerning the grave clothes, *"Loose Him, and let him go."*

In a practical sense, Jesus was telling those who were standing around to unwrap Lazarus from his grave clothes. There are always people in your life who want to help you, but they do not know how. My wife tried to help me, but I had shut her out. I had a few friends who were always in my corner, but I had cut myself off from them. I told everyone, "I'm fine. I'm doing good. All is well." That was a lie. I felt like this mess was my mess, and I had to clean it up on my own. I needed to come to a place of faith in God and to allow people to come close. There is healing in relationships.

In a spiritual sense, Jesus was speaking to the remnants of death. Lazarus was bound hand and foot, meaning he couldn't work, and he couldn't walk. His face was wrapped with a napkin so that he couldn't see, hear, speak, or even mumble a prayer. Whether there was a spiritual miracle or a physical one, the bottom line is that he was set free! All fear, remorse, apprehension, anxiety, stress, worry, doubt, and confusion—the effects, smells, and remnants of death—were all taken away. I speak the same to you. Perhaps you have been led to this book for such a time as this! Be loosed!

In the next few chapters, we will read about the road to restoration. But right now, before we take one step further, take a moment and turn your face to the earth and lift your heart to the Lord as a sacrifice. You may need to make some drastic changes but be open to the leading of the Holy Spirit. I pray for you right now in the name of Jesus, be free from this bondage of fear, of lack, of despair, of pride. Be free from all the bondage of sin. Be free from unforgiveness and harbored hurt. He whom the Son sets free is free indeed! AMEN!

David Cook

11

TURN AND REPENT

"Turn around!" The voice on my cell phone was insistent. I knew where I was going, but the GPS on my phone thought otherwise! I was headed home, but I had decided to make a stop at my favorite sporting goods store. As I passed by the turn toward home, my phone was quick to notice that I had gone off course, and it didn't hesitate to point that out to me. The GPS began instructing me how to get back on my route.

When the Global Positioning System first came out, I was a bit reluctant to get one. Eventually, though, I bought one and used it when I traveled for work or in areas where I needed some help with directions. Since then, the map services on cell phones have made the old GPS units obsolete, at least for me. I'm grateful for this technology, but if I decide to veer off the path it has set for me, it will let me know!

Naked and Ashamed

In Joel 1 and 2, the prophet describes a scene of an immense attack that left the city and the surrounding region depleted of resources. There was nothing left. Some scholars say that the destruction was so intense that even the bark was gone from the trees, and the doors were gone from their homes. Joel likens the attacking army to waves of locusts coming through the land.

Symbolism and metaphors carry deep spiritual meaning throughout scripture. Jesus taught using stories, and we follow the same model today in the modern era of inspirational preaching. Here is what I believe the Lord is saying to us today out of this desolate scene in Joel: when you fail, you stand stripped of everything—the enemy takes it all!

The bark missing from the trees signifies the loss of our protection in Christ. When our armor is off, we stand unprotected before our enemy, unable to fight or even defend ourselves. The doors missing from the homes signifies the violation of our privacy and our intimacy. When we fail, it can reach the deepest, most private parts of our lives and families. Our sin, our shame, our despair, our depression, our financial crisis, our marriage, our parenting style, our work ethic, our disheveled homes all stand uncovered before our enemy and before God—bare and exposed.

Like Adam and Eve in the Garden, we hide from God because we are naked and ashamed (Genesis 3:10). When we lose our covering, we are exposed before our enemy, before man, and ultimately before God.

David said in Psalm 51:3, "*...my sin is ever before me.*" The accuser of the brethren is all too happy to remind us of our sin on a continual basis. Those thoughts in our heads drive a wedge that further distances us from the love and goodness of God, which leads us to repentance. We tend to pull back from other people who remind us of our commitment to Christ, so we lack accountability. We look for solace in the wrong places and with the wrong people.

When we were pastoring in Western Ohio, I had to drive over to Columbus one afternoon to take care of some permits we needed for our septic system at the church and some other issues related to our church van. I stopped at a restaurant to grab a bite to eat before heading back home, and I was one of very few customers in the place.

The waiter took my order and came back by to check on me several times. He asked what brought me to Columbus and in to eat at such an odd time. I explained that I was a pastor, and I was there taking care of some church business. He came back by my table several times, to the point that it was noticeable. I could tell he was intrigued by the fact that I was a pastor, and he kept asking questions about our ministry, our church, and so on.

Finally, he asked if he could sit down and talk to me for a few minutes. As he did, he unfolded a story of rejection, pain, and hurt that tied directly back to his church. He told me he had been struggling with homosexual tendencies for several years. He was a member of a gospel singing group at his church that traveled all over the region and ministered in various venues. He said he went to his pastor and asked for help. He asked his leaders for prayer and deliverance ministry, but instead, he was blown off and rejected, even by his own family. Eventually, they put him out of the church, and his family turned their backs on him.

I am not justifying this man nor am I defending his sin. According to what he told me, he asked someone to help him with the battle he was facing, and they refused. He was visibly broken and wanted to find someone who would stand in faith, believing God with him to make a change. The lifestyle he was living was wrong, and he knew it, but he didn't have the power to change. He had lost faith in the church and even in God. It broke my heart. Tears welled up in his eyes when he said, "I don't want to go to Hell, pastor, but I can't change on my own. I'm so ashamed of how I'm living. I need help!" I prayed for that man, but I never saw or heard from him again.

Unfortunately, the church has been known at times to devour its own, just like this broken man I met that afternoon in a restaurant in downtown Columbus, Ohio. Because of this, sometimes people who are struggling within the church are fearful of seeking help from their brothers and sisters in Christ. However, I believe the cry of our culture is for authentic people—ones who have genuine faith and real love—who will cover one another, as did Noah's two sons in Genesis 9. We must take responsibility for our actions when we fail, lean on one another when we need it, and leave the rest up to God.

In the first eleven verses of Joel 2, he describes the attacking army as they are—an army of men storming the city. He talks about them climbing on the rooftops of the homes and buildings in the city. He tells of their structure, their organization, and how strong and intense they are. They march through the city, and the earth shakes and quakes. Fear grips the hearts of every man, woman, and child in their path.

If we are trying to come to grips with our failures and our sins, we must first realize that God is not mad at us. He has given us His Word. The fact that we feel distanced from Him is proof that we have not run so far from Him that His grace cannot reach us. He desires to pull us up and out. The Bible has a lot of *RE's* in it: *RE*pent, *RE*build, *RE*turn, *RE*store, *RE*fresh, *RE*count, *RE*vive. I'm so thankful for another chance!

Then, in verse 12, something amazing takes place. The Lord says, *"...turn and keep on coming to Me with all your heart, with fasting, with weeping, and with mourning [until every hindrance is removed and the broken fellowship is restored]"* (AMPCE). This call to repentance is what happened to me in the fall of 2014. I started looking for ways to reconnect with God, and I found some ways to do that at the church we were attending.

David Cook

My Turn

In the fall of 2014, our church offered a men's program. God had been dealing with my heart about making some changes. I was in an influential position in our community and felt that I needed to be attentive to how I was living. Furthermore, I felt that God began convicting me to TURN. So, in my heart—and very secretively—I started asking God to forgive me. I asked Him to help me. Then this men's program came about, and I decided to go, much to the surprise of my wife.

These meetings would mark the first time since we started attending our church in 2007 that I had spoken to anyone at church, other than in casual conversation. A few people realized that I was a coach at the high school, and I had talked to some people about the teams I coached and my work with kids, but not much more than that.

Throughout the fall semester in the men's program, we sat in groups and discussed a variety of topics. As I sat around the table week after week and talked to men—broken, Christian men—I realized that they were *just* as messed up as I was. They were all broken by life in some way. I realized that we all needed Jesus, regardless of how intense our stories were. I understood exactly what I had done to my family.

I cannot explain what happened to me at that point, other than with the following illustration. Let me take you forward to one afternoon in the early spring of 2016, when God showed me how He had worked in my life. I went outside and was looking around at our landscaping. I had a lot of work to do, so I got started pulling weeds. I dug down and moved some dirt out from around the root of one particular weed. I pulled gently on it until it started to break free and come out of the ground. As it came out, I noticed that dirt around the top of the weed began to move. The primary root was two to three times as long as the plant on top, and there were pieces of the root that went out in all directions from the main artery. Then, I reached down and covered the hole left by the root.

Sin is that way. It takes root deep in our hearts. The arteries that come off of the primary root affect multiple areas of our lives. Relationships, work, ministry, family, finances, behaviors—all are affected by the root of sin. Some things that we don't even know about are connected and affected by it. There is but one cure, and that's the blood of Jesus!

As I stood there looking at this thing, I heard the Lord say to me, "This is what I did in your life. I gently moved things around, and then I reached into the depths of your heart and pulled the junk out by the root. I took your roots of bitterness, fear, anxiety, failure, rejection, and sin out, and then I covered it back up."

Although I didn't fully understand it, I can tell you that in the fall of 2014, that's precisely what happened. God pulled it all out and cleared my mind of the constant struggle. He gave me peace that passes understanding, and I genuinely mean that. I knew, deep in my heart, I had been delivered and set free!

Like a car going off course and hearing the call from the GPS to "Turn Around," I turned around and what was once behind me was now in front of me. The areas of my life that I had left uncovered were now exposed and visible. I repented, turning 180 degrees in the opposite direction. As I did so, I could see that which I had once been pursuing, and it was in clear view.

The Apostle Paul said:

Brothers, I do not consider that I have made it my own. But one thing I do: forgetting what lies behind and straining forward to what lies ahead, I press on toward the goal for the prize of the upward call of God in Christ Jesus. (Philippians 3:13-14, ESV).

If nothing else, I decided I needed to turn toward God, and clarify in which direction my life would go from here on out. The first challenge I faced at that time was that of regret, but by God's gentle hand, He was restoring me and placing me in paths of right standing before Him.

Reflection

As we seek God for restoration in our lives, our families, our relationships, our marriage, our ministry, our finances, or any other area, we need to understand what we are asking. To restore something is to return it to the original design, the original purpose, and the original function.

As I described in the introduction to this book, when a classic car is restored, some original parts may be used, and some new or even remanufactured parts may be used. Original parts must be cleaned up and the effects of the environment knocked off, such as dust and rust.

The craftsman will fill holes on the body, clean the internal parts of the engine, and work tirelessly until the vehicle is in pristine condition. A restored car, then, has the best of the original parts functioning with new, and in some cases, improved parts. Restored vehicles may be even better in their restored state than they were in their original state. Each restored car has a history and a story behind how it got to this point.

Your story may have taken you through an endless cycle of fear and regret. Maybe you have failed your family and turned your back on God. Maybe you stepped out in faith and realized you were not ready, and you are sinking. If you've ended up dry, thirsty and visionless, TURN! That's the first step toward restoration!

Have you ever found yourself going the wrong way on a one-way street? Have you ever missed your turn on the way to an unfamiliar location? What do you do? You look for the earliest possibility to TURN AROUND! You stop moving in the direction you are going, and you TURN 180 degrees back in the opposite direction. That is what repentance is—turning around. It is only when you repent of your unbelief and your sin that things can begin to change, and you can be restored.

12

REVERSE YOUR COURSE

When I was 17 years old, I had a 1977 Oldsmobile Cutlass Supreme. It had a 350 engine and a four-barrel carburetor. It was white with a tan leather cover on the rear part of the car and tan interior—an awesome vehicle! Not long after I bought the car, the transmission started giving me problems, and the reverse went out. I could drive, but I had to park on a hill, or where I could pull straight through. Otherwise, I had to hang my leg out of the car and push it back from parking spaces. Eventually, I got a new transmission, and the car was good as new again. My point is this: sometimes it's hard to reverse circumstances yourself, but God can do exceedingly above all we could ever think or ask.

Around the spring of 2014, I started ushering once a month at our church. Shortly after that, our church started a security team. I was asked to volunteer based on my experience in the Marine Corps. I had served in this capacity while I was in Bible college, so I had some experience with it. I started connecting with people in the church, although I was still somewhat apprehensive about doing so. I had turned toward God, and I was beginning to believe that He would bless me as I continued to pursue Him.

Later that same year, God began to work deep in my heart. When I went to that men's meeting for the very first time, I knew something was going to change over the course of that semester-long program. It was a productive time of fellowship, and I don't mean a bunch of guys overeating on hot wings and watching football. Not that I am by any means opposed to that, but it was much more profound. God was working on our hearts.

I started reading a devotional on the Bible app on my phone every day. One day, I read Luke 18, a story about the Pharisee and the Publican (tax collector) who came to the temple to pray. I immediately identified with the tax collector. Tax collectors during this period in history were viewed as dishonest and despicable people. They would extort money from the people and abuse their authority. They were hated among their own people. Although people may have smiled at them in the streets, they were cut off from close relationships in their community.

The tax collector realized he was a sinner. He knew the wrongs he had committed. Even more so, he knew he needed God's forgiveness more than anything. I could identify with this man. I felt completely cut off from my wife and children. I felt alone and as if I had no significant relationships with anyone. I connected with him because I knew the condition of my own heart. I knew I had treated my family wrong, and I knew that the only cure for me was God's forgiveness. God showed me that He wanted my heart. If my heart was right, the service would follow.

Something shifted over the course of a few months, and the relationship I had with my wife changed DRASTICALLY for the better. God began doing a work in our marriage. We started to grow closer, and we became friends again. Our children were still kind of outliers in the home, but God was at work!

As Joel goes on, God gives the people a message of hope. He tells the people (I'm paraphrasing some here) it could be that God will reverse the sentence or stop the attacking army from advancing anymore. To *reverse* is to go 180 degrees in the opposite direction.

God says He will reverse the sentence. Think about that! Whatever it was, whatever we did, because of the cross, we can be saved. He overturned the punishment of sin and death and promised us eternal life. If we look at our life right now, in what ways have we failed God? Now, think of the results of that failure in this life and eternity, if we stay in that failure. Then, consider the course of our lives in the opposite direction of that result! That's God's promise to us right now! He's taking our debt and giving us a blessing. He's taking our death and giving us eternal life. He's taking our failure and giving us a future! God desires to TURN US AROUND!

The Means to Serve Him

Joel goes on to say that God will even leave a blessing behind to sustain and restore the people. The Amplified Classic Version reads this way in Joel 2:14: *"Who knows but what He will turn, revoke your sentence [of evil] and leave a blessing behind Him [giving you the means with which to serve Him]...."* He goes on in that verse to talk about sacrifices and offerings.

I had nothing left with which to serve God. I had no dream, no vision, no prophetic voice in my spirit guiding me, no money, no energy—nothing! When

Chapter 12: Reverse Your Course

I gave up, when I failed, it was all gone. I couldn't see or hear Him anymore. My vision to do great things in His name was not even on the radar. But God says He was going to REVOKE all that—even though I brought much of it on myself—and provide the means to serve Him.

I began feeling this stirring in my heart in 2015 to do public ministry of some sort again. I wanted to teach or preach again, but I wasn't sure how to move on that. I was fearful of it, and I told the Lord one day, "God, if you want me to do any public ministry, then YOU must open the door for me, and it has to be very clear and plain for me to do it!" I had to settle this stirring in my heart, but I wasn't sure how to go about it. I sat on that for several months and never uttered a word of it to anyone.

At the same time, in March 2015, my wife and youngest daughter, Ashley, came home and started pressing me to meet a little boy who was in my wife's class. Ashley has always had a tender heart, and she loves younger children. Maybe it was because she was our youngest child, but she seemed to avoid most of the turmoil in our family over the years. Her role in the change in our family is significant.

The little boy's name was Joseph, and he was living with his great-grandparents. Neither of his natural parents supported him, nor had they ever taken care of him. Joseph had some behavioral issues, and he needed a family. They started throwing around the term *adoption*. My immediate response was, "NO! I'm almost out of that game! I do not want to raise any more children!"

The reality of it was that I feared the adoption process. I knew people who had adopted children, and it had been an intense process. I was afraid of the background checks. I didn't want people to openly question through the adoption process the fact that I was still under a bankruptcy plan. Our marriage wasn't exactly stable yet, although it was improving. I did not think we were in a good place to take on another child.

However, the Lord began to work in my heart about Joseph. I agreed to meet him and to talk with his great-grandparents to discuss the possibility of helping out in some way. Meeting Joseph drastically changed the course of our lives forever, and I will talk more about his story later. Much of the blessing that God has brought into our lives came about as we took this step of faith.

As you begin turning toward God, you will find that He will start bringing things to you. Opportunities will come. People will come. Things will start to move in a new direction as you turn and keep turning and pursue Him!

We Need Relationships to Survive

Realizing that we cannot go through life alone requires that we first acknowledge our need for a Savior. I believed in God, and I knew Jesus was real, but I had to settle the issue of salvation first. I failed because I was isolated and alone. It was mostly my fault. However, when I sat in this men's group and listened to the guys around me talking about their struggles, I realized that only Jesus could fix any of us.

In Joel 2:12, in the Amplified Classic Version, Joel infers that broken fellowship is restored in this process. Almost immediately in the fall of 2014, our marriage began to heal. That to me was the most important relationship that I needed to address, aside from my relationship with Jesus. I had not genuinely communicated with my wife for several years before this. We had to have a blow-up or a significant fight in our marriage to reach a point of conversation.

Something clicked in my heart during that semester-long program, and I began to connect with God again. I started reading devotionals on my Bible App (thank God for technology, when used correctly). I began serving more at our church. I agreed to usher once a month because I could do it quietly. I began getting more involved in our security team. I eventually started doing scheduling for the security team, which created opportunities for me to meet and talk with other men in our church. I began to develop real relationships with Christian people, and more importantly, with my wife.

The enemies invading the land of Judah stripped them of their produce and prosperity. Judah's adversaries robbed them of their protection and invaded their privacy. As we saw in the previous chapter, the bark on the trees was gone, and the doors of their homes were destroyed.

There is power in relationships with other believers. After the flood, Noah was found uncovered. In Luke 15, Jesus tells us the story of a prodigal son. In both these instances, there were those who placed a covering on the exposed individuals.

In Genesis 9, two of Noah's sons walked into the room backward and covered their father when he was drunken. They didn't want to see what was going on with him, and they didn't need to talk about it. In Luke 15, the father came out looking for his lost son, placed a robe on him, covering him and the remnants of his past. Godly relationships provide covering and protection in our lives.

The cross is a tremendous example of how we relate to God and others. Jesus was lifted up on a vertical beam toward Heaven, symbolizing our need to look to Him. His arms were stretched out across a horizontal beam toward two thieves sentenced to death, one on each side. The horizontal cross beam symbolized our need for human relationships. In other words, the cross demonstrates a vertical relationship and a horizontal relationship. We need both to reach our fullest potential in Christ. We must establish our relationship with Him, and work to develop our relationships with other people in our lives.

You cannot connect with God and not connect with people. It is just not possible. As my heart began to change, and God began to show forgiveness toward me, I started to feel connected to others again. My fear of someone genuinely knowing me was diminishing.

In Joel 2:16, there is a call for assembly issued. The passage says, *"Gather the people...."* No one was exempt; God said to bring everyone. Men, women, children, the sick, the elderly, the leaders, the followers, the great men, and the men of low esteem: EVERYONE was to attend the assembly.

The enemy wants us to feel isolated. Why is that? If the enemy can isolate us, his next step is to push us into a place of discouragement where we are subject to the invasion of gnawing thoughts. Our first step to restoration must be realizing that we cannot live our life alone. God said in the beginning, *"...it is not good (sufficient, satisfactory) that the man should be alone..."* (Genesis 2:18, AMPCE). Subsequently, God created Eve to be a companion for Adam. We were not created to be isolated.

In 1 Peter 5:8, the Bible refers to our adversary, the Devil, as a prowling and roaring lion, seeking whom he may devour or destroy. A lion cannot catch a gazelle. Lions will isolate one gazelle out of the herd and run it until the gazelle is exhausted. Then, they can take the gazelle down and consume it. Our enemy makes a lot of noise, and he will try to isolate and drain us. Once he has us down, he'll try to devour us.

Reconnection

When God began working in my heart, he turned me toward my family first. The power of the Holy Spirit working in my home wholly overhauled our marriage. My wife and I were not communicating, and we were at odds to the point that I thought our marriage would not make it.

In the fall of 2014, something changed when God reached into the depths of my being and pulled the root of sin out. I felt it happen. I felt as though God was turning me inside out. For me, it wasn't an overnight or immediate experience; it happened over the course of a few months.

However, He began a fantastic work in me, and my marriage has never been the same since. Becca and I are the best of friends, and we enjoy all the time we can get together. She preaches the Gospel to me every single day, just by her presence in my life. Becca knows me, yet she chooses to love me. She sees my shortcomings, yet she stays by my side anyway. I'm honored to know someone as loyal and dedicated as she is.

The second part of this phase of restoration in my life had to do with my children. The two older children and I didn't have much of a relationship. My bond with them had deteriorated over the years to the point where I was not sure they'd ever speak to me again.

However, God began to change all of that in the fall of 2014. Today, my wife and I have a much better relationship. We talk all of the time about life, about ministry, about experiences we've had and shared. The same is true with our kids. We have grown in our relationship. Indeed, there is a level of maturity in their lives that contributed to this as well, but those things that were within my realm of control God began to lead me in and through.

The third part of this phase of restoration in my life came about in my connections to other people. I'm not even sure how it came about, but I reconnected with a terrific friend I knew from Kenya, and a pastor in Indiana who had introduced me to him back in 2001. I had not spoken to either of them since 2004, other than an email I had exchanged with my friend from Kenya in 2011. We reconnected in the spring of 2016.

When I saw these two men after so many years, something leaped inside me. I felt as if a part of me came alive that had been dormant for a long time. After that weekend, I met with the senior pastors at our church and began to share with them my experiences in ministry. I became more involved in my church, and I began to reconnect with other people I knew in ministry.

I reached out to one of the pastors who had been an overseer for our ministry in Ohio. The last time I had communicated at all with him, I had lied to him. I had told him that we were okay, and all was well, and I was happy to be rid of the ministry. It was all a lie. I was not doing well. My family was about to fall apart, and I was on the doorstep of financial ruin.

Emotionally, I was shattered and couldn't see my way through the fog of what I had allowed my life to become. I reached out to him again in January of 2017, and I apologized and told him the truth. He graciously accepted us, and we are growing our relationship with him and his beautiful family and church again.

We reconnected with another pastor from Kansas City, who attended Bible college with me back in the 1990s. It's been great to see what God has done in his life and ministry, and we are so excited to restore fellowship with him! We connected with two other pastors in St. Louis around the same time. My wife had worked for a significant ministry in St. Louis for nine years when we first moved here. She knew both of these pastors from her time there as well.

Since the time I graduated from Bible college in 1998, the school had gained additional accreditation and was now offering an associate's degree. Therefore, I inquired about returning to the college through their online program and completing the associate degree. I learned that I only needed to take four courses to complete the degree, so I did that, and God miraculously provided the tuition money!

I then connected with the organization where I had been ordained when serving in full-time ministry. In 2004, I said I wouldn't go back, and I wouldn't try to engage with them again. I just wanted nothing to do with my past, because I felt it was a hindrance to me professionally. However, I contacted them with the utmost humility and with an apologetic stance and asked if they'd consider reinstating my ordination. I wrote out my story and told them I had been wrong. I asked for forgiveness, and said that I understood if this was not possible. To my surprise, they reinstated me, and I am honored to reconnect with what we consider to be our home church yet again.

My middle daughter, Sarah, decided to attend the same Bible college I had attended. She started there in the fall of 2017. I took her to visit the church and the school in the spring of 2017. When I took her there for her first campus visit, it was the first time I had been on the campus in over 14 years. I had a fantastic visit with her there and was able to reconnect with so many wonderful people that I had cut out of my life.

Sarah had been healed at a Miracle, Healing and Victory Service at that same church in 2001 when she was a very small child. She couldn't hear anything under 100 decibels. In the service that night, when I was there as a struggling pastor with a few members of our church, God healed our little girl. We went back to the doctor a few weeks later, and all the testing proved the fact that God had healed her. We were on the ministry's television broadcast afterward, telling the story of Sarah's healing.

Now, we have been able to attend large events and meetings held at the main church in Ohio again, where I had once attended Bible college. Through these events, I met other pastors and reconnected with various elders in the church that I had known when we were there. In all, we had been a part of that ministry for about ten years, and I had walked away from all of it. It's been fantastic returning home!

God allowed me to restore regular communication with two other close friends that I had met in Bible college. They are solid guys, and both are firm believers. We talk about the things of God often. They are just great friends of ours who knew we were struggling but didn't understand the depth of it until now.

My friendship with my best buddy growing up has grown as well. He and I are both on the other side of 40 and looking at life much differently now. He went through a divorce some time ago, and I regret that he did so at a low point in my life, when I was not in any position to be much of an encouragement to him. We often talk about faith, family, children, home, and how it all measures up in the scope of eternity.

There are several other old friends and new friends that God has restored and added to my life. I've met so many wonderful people who love us just like we are. I commented in a membership class at our church once, saying, "I was a bitter man!" to which one of our associate pastors said, "Yes, you were!"

God not only restored my relationship with Him, but He restored my relationship with my wife, with my children, and with my friends. He also restored my love for and connection with His church! We serve as often as we can. We minister where we are called upon to minister. It is so awesome to see how He could use even a sinner like me.

Reflection

The priests were called to "...*weep between the porch and the altar*..." in Joel 2:17. The act of weeping between the porch and the altar signifies the emptiness the nation was experiencing. Because they were so consumed and broken, and because they had no means to serve Him, nor offerings to give, their tears became their sacrifice. Psalm 56:8 infers that God collects our tears, and He knows how many we've cried.

Luke 7 records the story of a woman bringing an alabaster box of costly perfume and pouring it on the feet of Jesus. She began to cry, wetting His feet with her tears and wiping His feet off with her hair. Some in the room felt the woman wasted the precious perfume oil. I don't think Jesus cared about the oil; I think the genuineness of her tears is what moved Jesus. Psalm 126:5 says, *"They who sow in tears shall reap in joy and singing"*(AMPCE). As we stand stripped, broken, defeated, depressed, and hurt, let us weep before the Lord. If we have no other sacrifice left, let our tears be our sacrifice before the Lord.

The Lord wants our hearts. We can give all the money we want. We can attend every church service, camp meeting, and conference on the calendar and still not receive what He has for us. Therefore, we are to continually turn to Him and offer ourselves as a living sacrifice.

The Message Bible presents this concept in very plain terms. Romans 12:1 reads this way: *"So here's what I want you to do, God helping you: Take your everyday, ordinary life – your sleeping, eating, going-to-work, and walking-around life – and place it before God as an offering."* We are to present ourselves to Him daily. In doing so, we keep coming to Him continually. As Joel 2:12 reads, *"Turn and keep on coming to Me with all your heart...."* God desires that we do that every day.

The next few verses begin to lay out hope for restoration. As you read them, you'll find it is a complete reversal of the destruction that took place in the land. God promises grain, which is good for food for man and beast, signifying His desire to attend to our physical needs. He promises grapes and juice, symbolizing the new wine of the Spirit, which He will later mention in this chapter, and which also refers to restored joy. Nehemiah 8:10 says, *"...the joy of the Lord is [our] strength."* Therefore, God restores both our joy and strength. Strength refers to power for living, for serving, for loving others, for work, for facing the enemy. Joy produces strength in our lives.

He promises that the people will no longer be a reproach among nations, which signifies that He will remove the fear of failure and fear of exposure from our lives. He goes on to say how satisfied the people will be with these blessings, symbolizing the restoration of PEACE in our life.

Where are you today? Are you standing stripped, exposed, ashamed and afraid because of what you have done and the repercussions of your actions and your failures? Are you wounded and bruised from letdown after letdown? Have you isolated yourself to the point where you feel abandoned and alone? God is calling you to WAKE UP! He wants to do a new thing in your life, but that begins with repentance and restored fellowship with Him, and reconnection with the body of Christ. May the Spirit of the Lord reach into your heart and show you His plan for your life.

13

ORDERLY RESTORATION

God is a God of order. In the account of creation, we see God working in a precise and orderly fashion. On day one of creation, God created light and separated the light from the darkness. On day two, He created the firmament, and *"divided the waters which were under the firmament from the waters which were above the firmament"* (Gen 1:7). On day three, God separated the waters from dry land and created vegetation and plants. On day four, He created the sun, moon, and stars. On day five, God created creatures in the sea, and He created birds in the air. On day six, He created animals and livestock, and Adam.

Notice the order: plants cannot grow without light and water. Animals cannot survive without plants and water. Adam was not able to survive without plants for food and water. All animals at that time were vegetarians, as was Adam. God even gave Adam a job, knowing that man needed work to occupy him. God gave him authority over all of it. He had a plan, and the plan followed an orderly flow.

Revelation 13:8 describes the ultimate plan of salvation and restored fellowship with God and states that Christ was crucified from the foundation of the world. Hebrews 4:3 says that all the works were finished from the foundation of the world. Matthew 13:35 speaks of how Jesus revealed things that were kept secret from the foundation of the world. Matthew 25:34 speaks of the place prepared for believers from the foundation of the world. So, from the beginning, God had a plan to restore man to Himself.

A New Covenant

When God made a covenant with Abraham, Hebrews 6:13 says, *"...because he could swear by no greater, he sware by himself."* Upon reviewing that story in Genesis 15, we see that God commanded Abram (his name hadn't been changed to Abraham yet) to take a heifer, a female goat, a ram, a turtledove, and a pigeon and offer them as a sacrifice. The animals were split in two, divided with one half on each side and a path of blood down the center.

In the custom of the day, this was called "cutting a covenant." At that time, if two people cut a covenant, they would split the animals as described, and walk through the blood together. The symbolism is that if either party backs out on their covenant, they were giving the other party the right to split them in two as they did with the sacrifices and the animals. In Genesis 15:17, the Bible describes the two parties that walked through the blood as " *...a smoking furnace, and a burning lamp....*" Abram wasn't involved in the covenant because he was capable of failing. Therefore, God swore by Himself, because He could not fail.

In consideration of orderly restoration, here's what we need to understand—God knew all of this was going to happen. He knows what we're going to do before we do it. We have a free will to choose. God had a plan for Adam if he didn't sin, and He had a plan for Adam, and subsequently for us, if he did sin. He knew Adam would sin, so He made a way for us.

Galatians 3:13-14 says:

Christ hath redeemed us from the curse of the law, being made a curse for us: for it is written, Cursed is every one that hangeth on a tree: that the blessing of Abraham might come on the Gentiles through Jesus Christ; that we might receive the promise of the Spirit through faith.

You see, God made a covenant with Himself, knowing we would need a blood path to restored fellowship with Him. God had given us a plan of salvation long before we ever took a breath on this planet.

Everything in God's Kingdom is predicated on Him being the Supreme Lord of our lives. Therefore, the first and most important thing is that we repent. Joel 2:12 he says, "*...turn and keep on coming to Me with all your heart...*"(AMPCE). Salvation is not something we have to pursue continually, but righteousness is. Once God apprehends our heart and saves our soul, then we must become a disciple or a disciplined follower of Jesus Christ. Discipleship occurs while in the fellowship of other disciples or disciplined followers of Christ. We cannot grow alone.

Therefore, once we seek forgiveness from God, we must allow Him to lead and guide us in what we should do next. Many times, there are practical steps we need to take.

The first thing I felt I had to do was to begin reaching out to my wife. That was the very first relationship that needed to be mended by the Lord after I repented. Second, I started reaching out to my children. I tried to let some things go that I chose to focus on before. In summary, I decided to offer as much grace *to* them as I wanted *from* them.

Third, I needed to begin reaching out to other people. I started to reconnect with people: my friends in Kenya, pastors I knew in ministry, Christian friends that I never realized I had, and my local church pastors. I felt I needed to come clean with all of these people and seek forgiveness and restoration. And here's the amazing thing: THEY ALL ACCEPTED ME! Even the ones I didn't think would accept me did. I went from feeling entirely alone to being surrounded by like-minded people who desired the same thing I desired—RESTORATION!

The Process of Suddenly

Restoration is a process. There is a process to everything in life. There is a process to win, a process to produce, a process to reproduce, a process of life—in all things, there is an order. Restoration is not any different. It comes back to priorities in life. The things that are the most important must be the things we address first.

In Joel 2:12-17, relationships were restored. First was the restoration of the people's relationship with God and then their relationships with each other. After they came together in one mind and with one goal, they sought the Lord with all their hearts, and God was able to take them on into what He had for them. There is a process to restoration. If we're serious about restoration, we have to trust the process.

I believe in miracles. I believe in instant healing and creative miracles. However, there is a process to *suddenly*. No one sees the tears at night. No one sees the pain in our body and in our life. No one else understands how low we have gone. No one sees us when we're crawling in the dirt and the mud or hiding in shame. But when the instant happens—when suddenly comes—there's no shortage of celebration! But we know better than anyone where we were and from where He brought us. Restoration appears sudden to the casual observer, but there is a process to get to a *suddenly* moment.

When we compare Joel 1:4 and Joel 2:25, the attacking insects are not listed in the same order. Here is the order they attack:

1. Palmerworm – Gnawing Locust
2. Locust – Swarming Locust
3. Cankerworm – Licking Locust
4. Caterpillar – Consuming Locust

However, in Joel 2:25 the order is different. Here is the order of restoration:

1. Locust – Swarming Locust
2. Cankerworm – Licking Locust
3. Caterpillar – Consuming Locust
4. Palmerworm - Gnawing Locust

These terms present a picture of the orderly process of restoration. When God showed me this in 2003, I thought it had to do with the struggles we had faced in ministry for the previous five years. I thought God was going to open things up for us and allow us the opportunity to be restored and moved into the place He had for us. However, in 2014, I realized that I had to walk through this on a much deeper level.

I still believe that all of this had to do with our struggle in ministry, but I had to go through the process. Repenting and taking steps to reconnect with my wife and children were only the beginning of the process of restoration. The adoption of Joseph was a continuation of the process, and the reentry into ministry was the culmination of the process. Like Adam, I believe the opportunity was there to do it God's way at that time. However, God knew I wouldn't go that route, so He had a plan for me, and He has one for you, too.

A few years after I quit the ministry, I burned everything I could burn. I burned all my study notes, my journals, my sermon notes, my contact list—everything! I even gave away my books to another pastor in our area. I wanted to remove it all from my life.

In 2014, I started rereading Joel 1 and 2. I recall thinking, "I sure wish I had my notes from when I preached this sermon in 2003." But, the Lord brought to my remembrance what I had preached on in 2003 concerning this passage. Haggai 2:9 says that *"the glory of this latter house shall be greater than of the former...."* I believe God has given me even more truth and revelation from this passage now than I had then.

Reflection

God is a God of order, and He made a way for us to be restored to right standing before Him through Christ. Man had very little to do with any of the definitive works of God. The plan of God was complete before time began. God knows us better than we know ourselves, but He will not impose Himself on an unwilling heart.

All the things that I can attribute to the work of the Lord in my life have come about because I surrendered my will to His divine conviction. God is not looking to harm us; He is looking to restore us. If you've failed, if you've blown it, if you've backslidden, if you're currently living in sin—God loves you! Jesus paid the price for you. Here's the beauty of it: it requires only your acceptance of His mercy in your life. Repent, and start pursuing Him today. Watch what God will do in your life!

David Cook

14

RESTORING VISION

In Joel 2:25, we see restoration beginning in Israel. God said, *"I will restore or replace for you the years..."*(AMPCE). Now, this thing is going to start getting exciting! I lost ten years with my children. I lost ten years of ministry. I lost ten years with my wife. I lost ten years of being a true disciple of Christ! I did it, and I blame no one but myself. I gave up, I quit and allowed the devil to isolate me and rob me of my vision and my ability to hear from God.

What God has shown me is that once restoration begins, it seems to happen at a rapid pace, at least on the surface. However, like the woman with the issue of blood, there were years spent living in the negative circumstances, trying to find a way to be made whole. Once we reach the point where our own resources are gone, healing and restoration seem like a far-fetched notion at best. But when we encounter the Master, it appears to happen suddenly!

The years that the swarming locusts ate are the first to be restored in Joel 2. This phase of restoration refers to our vision and our ability to hear from God. Years ago, I heard a definition of prayer, and it was something like this: prayer is communing and conversing with, asking and receiving from God.

How can I move if I cannot see? How can I pray if I cannot hear Him respond? The first thing we need to realize is our need for a Savior. I had to come face-to-face with the state of my spiritual health, and it was not good. Repentance opened my eyes to see exactly what I had done, and what I had allowed to happen in my life and family.

Psalm 126:1 says, *"When the Lord restored the fortunes of Zion, we were like those who dream"* (ESV). A dream existed at one time in my life—a vision for the future—but it seemed dead to me.

However, when God begins to restore our lives, He leaves nothing undone. The very first thing He will do is restore our vision for the future. He shows us what is possible again! The view of possibilities produces hope. Hope has to do with the expectation of favorable things coming about in our lives.

If you've lost your dream, you can DREAM AGAIN! I believe God challenges us in these times to look at what's possible and dream big. You'll still have to walk it out, but if you have a vision, a goal, a dream for your life and future, hold on to it as you press forward!

I repented and began seeking God through prayer, reading His Word, and serving in our local church, but I still had no vision for the future. I was trying to get through each day. However, about six months after I started attending a men's program at our church, I began to feel God stirring my heart to something, but I didn't know what.

Looking for a Common Goal

I knew my family needed to identify a rallying point, something that we could all get behind. In the spring of 2015, we encountered the little boy who needed a home. When we met Joseph, he had just turned five years old. He had some behavior problems, but we just fell in love with this little boy. He lived with his great-grandparents at the time.

They had approached the school where Becca and I worked, asking if they knew of anyone who would consider adopting Joseph. They were concerned that if either of them was to pass away, Joseph would be left with no one and would end up in state custody and foster care. After much debate and discussion in our home, we started the process of trying to adopt him, or at least becoming his legal guardians. We encountered obstacles along the way, but we felt God had given us the vision to do this.

My family came together under a unified vision for the future. It wasn't all just about Joseph, but that was the spark that ignited the dreams in each of our hearts. All three of my children started college around the same time, a dream I had carried for each of them since they were born. They've all since turned to God with all their hearts, and they are all serving the Lord today.

Vision promotes vision. Dreams encourage dreams. Goals promote goals. It's hard to get around a visionary person and not walk away inspired to dream! I believe that when we shared with our family the vision of adopting Joseph, they were inspired in their own lives to dream.

Pioneering Spirit

In the summer months of 2016, my school district had started looking into signing a contract with a company to provide uniforms. I went to visit one of the companies from which we were accepting a proposal. They invited several of us over to their site, gave us a tour of their operation, and took us out to lunch.

When I walked into the place, I recognized vision. The owner of the company was, in a sense, a pioneer. He had started the business in his garage and had grown it to what we saw that day. He had a warehouse, several screen-printing machines, and a large staff of people to run the business. He had built the new facility and had done all of the interior work himself, along with his employees. There was a feeling of new beginnings, and I wanted that for my life again.

We started the adoption process. Over the next two-and-a-half years, we had seven continuances for a court date, until we finally went in to have the case heard on the eighth court date. We had our case assigned to three different judges, before being placed in the court where the case would finally be presented. It seemed as though we would never realize this vision. But a pioneer continues, looking at what's possible, regardless of the obstacles they face. That is precisely what we did.

In the summer months of 2016, Joseph received a diagnosis of Level 2 Autism Spectrum Disorder. At this point, we became more passionate about bringing this to a close and getting Joseph the help he so desperately needed. Our children rallied to support us, and God began working intensely in their lives as well. We bolstered our vision to get this done, and decided somehow, someway it would come to pass. I had no idea how we could afford to pay for it, but we all agreed that if God brought him to us, then God would provide.

I knew God brought Joseph to us, but I never felt that was all. I was working hard at the school, trying to improve our athletic programs and be an example of a Christian man for my athletes and my family. However, I felt there was still more. The Holy Spirit was working in my life and igniting something that was buried deep under all of my perceptions and failures. So, I began to seek God about returning to ministry. I just had this stirring in my heart that wouldn't subside. It only grew stronger as I pressed into God's Word. I felt compelled to seek God concerning ministry.

David Cook

But Wait ... There's More

We've all seen the infomercials. They have a fantastic product they are selling that will make every aspect of your life so much better if you would just buy the product. There is entirely no way you can live without it. Everything from cookware to sunglasses to pillows to exercise and diet programs, if you order their product and pay $9.95 shipping and handling, your life will be all the better for it. You will look like a supermodel, sleep like a rock, and never be blinded by bright sunlight again. And near the end the infomercial, the announcer almost always says, "But wait! There's more! If you call today, we'll double your order and send you not one, but TWO of our amazing widgets! Just pay separate shipping and handling."

I felt the same way when we were going through the initial stages of our adoption. I knew God brought Joseph to us, but there just had to be something else. Becca and I had a dream for our lives. We had a dream for the ministry to which God had called us. I remember during the early stages of the adoption thinking, "Lord, is this all? Do you have more for me to do?"

As we reconnected with people that we had not even so much as heard a word from in 14 years, we had confirmation after confirmation of what we were both feeling in our hearts concerning our future. My friend from Kenya even said to me, "Brother, this is an answer to prayer! We have prayed for you every day in Kenya! I rebuked the devil and prayed for restoration to the ministry God has called you to."

I'm amazed that the God of the entire universe is concerned about us as individuals, and that He takes time to care about you and me. In Matthew 6, Jesus said that we should take no thought for tomorrow, what we should eat or wear. He said that God makes sure that every single bird has food to eat, even though they do not grow food or work the land. He went on to say that God adorns the lilies in the field in such splendorous beauty that nothing compares to it. We serve a BIG, AWESOME, AMAZING God! He cares about us right where we are!

I came to the realization in the spring of 2016 that God had orchestrated all of this. He knew what I'd do before I did it. He knew I'd walk away. He knew I'd reach a point in my life where I felt like I was lost and alone. He knew that I'd turn back to Him. He knew I'd one day start asking Him if it were possible to be used in the work of the ministry again. He knew my friend from Kenya would be within driving distance in April and May of 2016, and He knew I'd find him and visit.

It was during that visit when God began speaking to me more than ever. We went to dinner with the pastor and the bishop from Kenya, and as we talked, the glory of God was all around our booth. That was when I felt flooded with vision and began hearing God's voice clearly about the future of my family.

It's never just about us, but God is concerned about us. The Apostle Paul referred to this life of faith as a *"mystery,"* meaning it's not something to be figured out in our natural mind, but we use all of our faculties to try to understand it. I am so grateful He found me and gave me a second chance! I'll never understand why, but I'll do my best to be thankful.

For about a year before seeing my friend from Kenya in April of 2016, I had felt a stirring to be involved in some sort of public ministry—perhaps even preaching—again. I genuinely wanted to go back to Kenya, if only to work and help out with their ministry for a few weeks.

However, I had nowhere to preach and no means to do any kind of public ministry. After all, who would want to hear what I had to say? I was washed up, dried up, and used up. I hadn't preached in years. In 2016, I told the Lord, "If you want me to do any sort of public ministry, any preaching, then you open the doors for me to do so." I then gave God the names of specific pastors and churches I wanted Him to open to me. Since that time, He has. Much to my amazement, God has worked in the way I asked Him to.

God's Desire to Partner with Us

The Lord will include you in His work. In John 9, we read an account of Jesus healing a blind man. This event took place on the sabbath day, which of course upset the religious crowd. When Jesus moves in our lives, it will not be accepted by all. But those to whom He sends us will embrace it. In verse four, Jesus says something very interesting: *"We must work the works of him who sent me while it is day"* (ESV). There is no mention of anyone else's involvement in the miracle other than Jesus and the blind man. He didn't call together a prayer circle or ask others to stretch their hands toward the blind man. It was just Jesus showing His authority over the situation and the blind man receiving it.

Even still, Jesus says, *"we must work the works...."* I believe He was setting an example and giving us some insights into what was to come. In Acts 1:8, Jesus said, *"You will receive power when the Holy Spirit has come upon you."* In John 14:12, Jesus said, *"...whoever believes in me will also do the works that I do; and greater works than these will he do…"* (ESV). We are to be partners with Him, and our vision for life must fit within the larger framework of His vision for humanity.

It is the will of God that ALL should be saved! He came to give life and life more abundantly than we could ever imagine. I cannot believe God would pay the price He did for us to leave us in bondage—to leave us broke, depressed, diseased, poor, hurting, weak, addicted, afflicted or distressed. He came to set us FREE from all the power of sin in our lives. Glory to His name! He will restore the years of vision that the enemy stole from us, even when we allowed it to happen.

I was praying (the lazy way) once and said this: "God, You know what I need, so take care of it for me, please!" I felt the gentle nudge and heard that still small voice in my spirit saying, "That is true, I do know what you need. But I want you to tell me. Declare the need met, as I have given you the authority to do. I love you, and I want you to come into agreement with my Word over your life, your family, and your ministry."

Wow! I can employ the Word of God out of my mouth and frame my future, as I come into agreement with His Word! Lest you believe this is not Biblical, Isaiah 43:26 says, *"Put me in remembrance…"* (ESV). God is saying, "I give you full freedom to make your requests known to me. Plead your case on your behalf. Remind me of My Word. Remind me of my promises to you."

Reflection

You and I need to have vision to survive. I can tell you it will be ugly at first. When God revealed the state of my heart to me, it was sickening. BUT He is gentle. He is loving. He is good. Proverbs 3:12 says, *"For whom the Lord loveth he correcteth.…"* Even His corrections are good. It's His goodness that leads us to repentance in the first place. When our eyes open, and we can see the state of our life in the light of His goodness, He will begin to heal our hearts. He will pull out that which does not belong, as we submit to Him. He will start to restore His vision in our hearts.

What is it that God gave you, that you turned your back on because of failure and fear? Was it a plan for a career? A goal for your family? Did you have a dream for a business? You see, God CAN and WILL restore your vision as you submit your life to Him. My prayer for you right now is that the eyes of your heart be opened to see your current state, but, more importantly, to know the plan God has for you. Lord, restore their vision in Jesus Name!

David Cook

15

RESTORING PROVISION, PROTECTION AND PRIVACY

Due to a series of wrong decisions in my life, I was now facing the very thing I feared most: being homeless. One of my biggest fears growing up was to end up broke and unable to provide for my family. I thought I had done everything I could to make sure that didn't happen.

My wife and I had struggled financially in our home as far back as I can remember. We had periods that were more intense than others, but it all culminated in 2013 when we went bankrupt. My situation was a culmination of events; it wasn't sudden. It was an area that had plagued me my entire life: I made bad decisions about money.

In Joel 2:25, the second locust listed was the cankerworm, or licking locust. The cankerworm has a firm grip and can sit for long periods of time, consuming every possible food source in its path. To bring that into focus, this insect represents the sins and weights in our lives that won't go away just because we want them to. I didn't want to file bankruptcy, and I certainly didn't want to become homeless. Things were heading that direction anyway.

In Luke 9:37-42, Jesus delivered a little boy bound by a demon. The father of the boy came to Jesus and said, *"...I begged your disciples to cast it out, but they could not"* (v. 40, ESV). In Matthew's account of the same story, the disciples were perplexed about why they could not cast the devil out of the boy.

Jesus replied to them saying, *"Howbeit this kind goeth not out but by prayer and fasting"* (Matthew 17:21). Although some translations omit this particular verse, I believe it speaks to the power of prayer and fasting when dealing with afflictions, infirmities, constant spiritual attacks, and generational curses. Fasting does not move God, but it pushes the flesh into submission to God, and promotes strength in our innermost being, our spirit man.

This phase of restoration has to do with spiritual and physical provision. In the land of Judah, their enemies consumed all their sustenance. The land was plagued by an immense and intense attack, followed by drought-like conditions. Therefore, they were in a low state. In Joel 1:14, God commanded the prophet to *"sanctify...a fast, call a solemn assembly...."* They had to revive their spirit and cry out to God for restoration.

Filing bankruptcy and facing homelessness, we were in a low state. We needed a solemn assembly. Due to poor planning, a lack of communication in our house, and my rebellious heart toward God, my wife and I never talked about much other than surface stuff. We never really communicated.

Right after we moved into our home, I had been living however I wanted to and doing whatever I pleased. I would hang out with my friends and leave my wife at home. We didn't talk or communicate. The lack of communication was a problem that had plagued us for a long, long time. The financial issues were just a symptom of a much larger issue.

She didn't trust me. I had female friends, and in some of those friendships, I had allowed emotional ties to take place. My wife knew it, and her trust level was low. I let it happen, and she was always questioning my devotion to her. That's why she was afraid to tell me about the financial woes that were looming.

Man of Many Masks

Over the years, my wife and I had exchanged many negative words. In my mind, I had destroyed my reputation as a husband and a father. Whether we want to admit it or not, we all talk to ourselves all day, every day. In my case, my self-talk was always negative. I would continually run myself down in my mind. Words like *failure* or *stupid* or *dumb* were continuously rolling around in my head. I may have needed therapy, but like most people in our culture, I had become very good at putting on a mask.

We wear masks to church. We wear a different mask at work. We wear another one in the community, at the grocery store, or at our kids' little league games. The reality is that no one knows us like we know ourselves, other than God, who knows all things. Consider how many people are sitting in church pews every single week who are bound by prescription drug addictions, pornography addictions, sexual addictions, addictions to caffeine or sugar, addictions to unrealistic spending and consuming, addictions to technology and social media or any other thing that exalts itself in our lives.

Chapter 15: Restoring Provision, Protection and Privacy

It's not just the stuff that's illegal that binds people. A good test to see if such a thing binds you is to try to go a few days without it. Trust God, and see if you can make it without it. Fast coffee for 21 days and see if your flesh can make it. Give up your favorite dessert for a week. Don't log in to any form of social media for a week. If you want to know if you're bound, give it up and see how your flesh responds.

The use of many masks is crippling to believers and will rob us of our authority and power. The devil knows full well what he's doing. It is somewhat like multitasking. If you are juggling too many tasks at one time, you may forget which things are a priority to finish first. You might forget that you're at church and cuss like you do at the water cooler at work. You may forget you are at your kid's little league game and try to pray over the fast food meal you snagged on your way to the game. Keeping all of that compartmentalized is hard. It puts undue pressure on you, and your mind can't keep up at times.

The beautiful thing about realizing you've blown it is the liberty to throw all the masks away. Not that I feel I need to rehash my failures, but there is healing and freedom in telling someone else how Jesus set me free. I don't have to wear a mask!

In John 8, the religious leaders brought a woman caught in adultery to Jesus. They placed her in their midst and backed away, ready to stone her according to the law of Moses. Jesus responded to them in verse 7 saying, *"Let him who is without sin among you be the first to throw a stone at her"* (ESV). The Bible says that one by one they dropped their stones to the ground and walked away. The woman was left there alone at Jesus' feet. Jesus asked her where her accusers were now. Then he told her, *"Neither do I condemn you; go, and from now on sin no more"* (v. 11, ESV). Jesus removed this woman's mask forever. She no longer had to live in fear and hiding.

We can't continue to condemn the actions of people who are struggling, and we must learn to forgive ourselves. Jesus isn't ashamed of us, and He will receive our cry for help and repentance. He will replace our shame with His Divine confidence! Our sin is not greater than His sacrifice, and neither is the sin of any other person we encounter. If you think you may have overextended God's grace, then you indeed would not be reading this! His grace is greater than all our sin!

The grip of hidden sin and deep emotional wounds is very tight. Like the cankerworm, they will hold on for a long time and eat away at your very soul. It requires *repentance* and *accountability* to truly be set free from hidden sins and wounds, mixed with a whole lot of love and support. It saddens me to think how many people are in churches right now, and they are bound. It is as if we refuse Jesus' sacrifice. There is no question that preachers must not condone sin from the pulpit. However, we have to find a way for people to receive the healing and forgiveness they so desperately need.

It Has to Change

In March of 2013, I felt so ashamed and so embarrassed by what my life had become. The wounds in my heart sparked behaviors in my life, and I hurt the people I loved most. Like the Psalmist David wrote in Psalm 51, over the next several months the reality of what I had done to my marriage and my family was ever before me. In the spring of 2014, one year into the bankruptcy, I determined that I had to change. I started seeking opportunities to do just that.

My wife started working at the school where I worked, but in a different building. She took a pay cut, but it was all right. She didn't have to drive as far, and we felt like it would be good to have her close to home. In the fall of that year, God began to open my eyes, and He showed me what had gripped my life for so long.

As I kept turning to God's Word, I found out that He didn't think ill of me. He loves me with an undying love. It all seemed so elementary, but yet profound. The Amplified version of Philippians 2:6-7 says:

Who, although being essentially one with God and in the form of God [possessing the fullness of the attributes which make God God], did not think this equality with God was a thing to be eagerly grasped or retained, But stripped Himself [of all privileges and rightful dignity], so as to assume the guise of a servant (slave), in that He became like men and was born a human being.

He left the royalty and lavishness of Heaven to become a man and die for you and me!

So, my speech had to change. My personal view of myself had to change. The deception of the enemy that caused me to believe I was alone, and without any support structure, had to change. After all, if Jesus was willing to suffer for

Chapter 15: Restoring Provision, Protection and Privacy

me so that I could inherit eternal life, why stay the way I am? I needed to relearn what His Word had to say and begin believing that. When I say learn it, I mean get it in my innermost being, not just my head. I know the Bible, but I didn't have it hidden in my heart.

God gave us His Son as a sacrifice for our sin so that we could have eternal life. Think about that! Eternal life doesn't start when you die, or it wouldn't be eternal. Eternal life begins now! Therefore, He is concerned about how we live while we are on this planet. He died to forgive our past, redeem our present, and secure our eternal future.

I began fasting one day a week, in conjunction with our church's corporate prayer gathering on Wednesday nights. I started by giving up my favorite drink—coffee. I gradually progressed in this to the point I was giving up a meal or two, and sometimes going the whole day fasting, consuming only water. My spirit man came alive as I took control of my life through prayer and fasting. The grip of the cankerworm was beginning to loosen, and God was beginning to move powerfully in my heart.

The things that grip us tightly are the most detrimental to our growth as a believer. Hidden sins, past hurts, or habits we can't seem to break all limit our ability to walk in the authority for which Jesus paid a high price. Romans 6:4 says that we walk in the *"newness of life"* (ESV). Ephesians 2:6 says that God *"...raised us up with him and seated us with him in the heavenly places in Christ Jesus"* (ESV). Where is that seat located? Ephesians 1:21 says that it is *"far above all rule and authority and power and dominion, and above every name that is named, not only in this age but also in the one to come"* (ESV).

Reflection

The act of prayer or the engagement in fasting just for the sake of doing so will not change much. God is not moved by our vain repetitions nor is He moved by self-punishment. God responds to our heart. Psalm 51:17 says, *"The sacrifices of God are a broken spirit: a broken and a contrite heart, O God, thou wilt not despise."* As you turn in your innermost being, and you cry out to God from a posture of brokenness, He responds with love and acceptance.

People will let you down, and they will hurt you. You may make choices and decisions that end up costing you dearly. There could be issues that lingered on into your life and family from generations before you. All of this may grip your very soul and suffocate you and stifle your ability to grow and hear from God.

I have always enjoyed exercising. I have lifted weights since I was twelve years old. For ten years, I trained hundreds of young athletes, teaching them how to lift, the importance of proper nutrition and rest, and promoting the notion of consistency. Sporadic exercise is not enough to change your body or your overall health. What changes your body is consistency in your exercise routine, diet, and lifestyle.

The same may be said of finances. A savings account will not grow by one deposit. Credit scores will not improve by just paying our bills for one month. For money to grow or for our financial situation to improve, we must be consistent in our financial activities.

In like manner, some things will only be broken off our lives through consistent prayer and fasting. As I began to seek God, I realized quickly that I had to do it consistently. Demons will not leave just because we tell them to. We cannot break years of sin, generational curses, or perpetual bad decisions by a thirty second prayer before we eat dinner. In my life, I had reached a point of desperation where nothing I tried worked. Finally, I cried out to God, and He answered me! I realized that what I had been doing over and over had to change. I had to change, and I had to become consistent doing some different things. Consistency is only birthed over time.

What grips you? What is it that limits your movement? Sure, you can do some things, but you hit the same wall over and over and over. What is that wall? Is it a sexual sin? Is it a deep emotional wound you're afraid to admit? Is it a disease, or perhaps your family history? Jesus broke the curse of sin, so you and I do not have to stay that way. I urge you now, change that which you have done consistently, and fervently cry out to God every single day! Right now, I pray that the shame that has gripped your life breaks away from you in Jesus' name! Be RESTORED!

16

RESTORING FREEDOM

My wife's grandmother was a Christian—a real Christian. She had worked in the banking industry years ago and retired as a vice president of the bank that had employed her. She was one of the first women in St. Louis to reach the executive level in any industry at a time when the glass ceiling was much lower than it is today.

She was a woman of prayer; she prayed fervently every day. She was a tither and a giver—she always told me that the Lord had blessed her and her husband, who died just four years before her, because they supported their local church and gave to missions regularly. She knew how to hear from God, and knew how to, as the old-timers would say, grab hold of the horns of the altar and not let go until an answer came from the throne of God!

She came to visit us twice in 2015 before she died. She was 89 years old and just as sharp as ever. She was sitting at my table in May of 2015. She reached over and took me by the hand and said, "I believe God brought Joseph to our family. Dave, I'm going to pay for Joseph's adoption. Everything you need for it, I'm going to pay for the whole thing."

I said to her, "Grandma, you don't have to do that. I'll work it out." I was planning to work an extra job over the summer months to pay for it.

She responded to me, "That's not your choice. God brought Joseph to our family, and I want to see to it that his future is secured."

And she did! She paid for everything: legal fees, court fees, background checks, home study fees, new smoke alarms, plug covers for the outlets in our house, safety latches for our cabinets—EVERYTHING we needed to get the process moving. God came through and provided for Joseph. Psalm 68:6 states that God sets the solitary in families, and we believed that was happening for Joseph.

The Caterpillar Is Losing Its Grip

The caterpillar was the next type of locust mentioned in Joel's prophecy of restoration. This was the stripping and consuming locust. After we filed for bankruptcy in 2013, we went through several difficult months trying to work things out. By the spring of 2014, things started to settle down in our home. We still had no savings, and we were living from month-to-month (our school pays our salaries monthly). I had worked a certain amount of giving into the monthly budget, and I did what I could to tithe or at least get close to tithing.

It seemed like we couldn't get ahead. Every few months we encountered a major issue with a vehicle or with something breaking down in our house. How could we expect to help Joseph when our own financial house was not in order? After all, it takes a lot of resources to raise a child.

Sometimes we must do what we can do at the place where we are. God was stirring my heart at the time we met Joseph, and we felt like we were stabilizing to the point that we could help him. God is looking for people who are willing. You can play with the steering wheel in a parked car all you want, but you won't make any progress toward a destination until you pull away from the curb. We felt like we just needed to take a step and see what God would do. If we were wrong, it would be evident.

When God begins to take you through this phase of restoration, you will find your covering restored. That thing that once embarrassed you is no longer an issue, because it's under the blood. God will begin adding and rebuilding relationships in your life that will cover your inadequacies and deficiencies. Those things that once consumed all of your increase start to be replaced by things that add value to your life. The shame of your past then becomes a part of God's beautiful testimony of restoration in your life. I knew that if anything good came from my mess, it had to be from the Lord.

Indeed, there was more to our restoration than just financial miracles, but money was a part of it. Lest we believe that money is evil, we must understand that Ecclesiastes 10:19 says that money answers all things. It isn't the money that's evil but rather the love of money, or greed, that produces evil in the hearts of humanity (see 1 Timothy 6:10).

We began connecting with people who covered us in prayer, through our local church, and through others we had known while we were in ministry. There were opportunities for us to reciprocate and add to other's lives as well—anything alive has intake and outflow—so we had to be giving and receiving. It was about a two-year process, but God began to add to our lives little by little.

Chapter 16: Restoring Freedom

Joseph was such a huge part of what the Lord did for us during this time. The way our family responded to Joseph coming into our lives was terrific! Our restoration process was underway, and the provision for Joseph from Becca's grandmother was an important part of that process. Sadly, she passed away on the second day of school in 2015. We were hoping and praying that she would get to see the outcome of our adoption case, but the Lord called her home.

We went to court in August of 2015, and Joseph's natural father showed up to contest the adoption. And so began our two-and-a-half-year long fight over the future of Joseph's life.

The financial hardships that had gripped us throughout our marriage seemed as if they would not let go. However, we started to experience one small miracle after another. We increased our giving, as we progressed toward the final year of our bankruptcy plan. When we look back over this time, we can see how God provided again and again. The grip of financial pressure was breaking from our lives. There was a shift moving us from survival mode to a life of significance, where we could make a difference in our family and community. We never lived a day we didn't have to trust God, but sometimes our circumstances clouded our ability to have faith.

The cankerworm and the caterpillar have a tight grip. Like a python, they squeeze until life expires. It was like a constant choking of our joy, our happiness, our health, our finances, our relationships, our spiritual walk—every area of our lives.

When you are squeezed, whatever is inside of you will come out. I believe that God allowed me to go through this to squeeze every ounce of foolish pride and unbelief out of my heart until I had to trust Him. He knew that at some point in my life, I had received faith. It was in my heart, but all of life's pressures and the circumstances I was facing covered the seed of faith in my life. The squeezing pushed all of that to the surface so that the faith planted in my life years before could begin to grow and produce.

It Just Doesn't Fit Anymore

In Isaiah 10:27, God says, *"And it shall come to pass in that day, that his burden shall be taken away from off thy shoulder, and his yoke from off thy neck, and the yoke shall be destroyed because of the anointing."*

One day as I was dressing, I tried to button the top button on my shirt. I said to my wife, "The dry cleaners shrunk my shirt."

She just laughed. "I don't think the dry cleaners is the problem," she said. In other words, I had gotten a little chunky, and the shirt didn't fit anymore because of the fatness of my neck.

Once we begin to move forward in restored faith, things will begin to change. Isaiah 10:27 says that the " ...*yoke shall be destroyed because of the anointing.*" The word that is translated *anointing* may also be translated as *fatness*.

Once the restoration process begins, it gathers a momentum of its own. It follows a distinct path, outlined in this verse, by which we can gauge our progress through the process:

- The burden is coming off. You will not need to fight this battle. God is going to lift that heaviness and give you the garment of praise (Isaiah 61:3).

- As the yoke is removed from your neck, the choke hold will be released. However, if all God does is take it off, you may be tempted to put it back on.

- The yoke will be destroyed because of the anointing. Better yet, it will be destroyed to the point that it cannot be used again.

The first part of Isaiah 10:27 says that the burden will be removed, and the yoke taken off our neck. If we stop there, then we have a problem. Consider—for a moment—a plow, a yoke and a pair of oxen. When the farmer finished plowing for the day, the oxen were allowed to rest. The farmer unfastened the yoke, took it off their necks, and put it away to be used again later. If the yoke is removed and not destroyed, it can be used again and again.

But God didn't stop there! He said the yoke will be DESTROYED because of the fatness in our lives.

When God breaks the grip of the cankerworm and the caterpillar off our lives, we will understand what Paul meant in Romans 6:4 when he said that: " ...*we too might walk in the newness of life...*" (ESV). It's a brand-new day! The yoke is DESTROYED and that which once bound you is now gone.

We can't say the same things we used to say. We can't do the same things we used to do. We may need to change our profile picture on our social media accounts and find some new friends to hang around with on the weekends. We can't put the yoke back on, because it doesn't exist in our life anymore!

When we come into contact with the Christ, the Anointed One and His anointing, He will set us free. John 8:36 says, *"So if the Son sets you free, you will be free indeed"* (ESV). The Anointed One and His anointing, dwelling on the inside of us by the power of the Holy Spirit, will break into pieces the yokes that once held us captive! We CAN'T stay the same!

As a result of this, God will begin to restore our reputation. You see, when I gave up, when I backslid, I cashed in all my chips. I had no reputation left. However, when God restores things, when God accelerates time, He brings it all back to where it was supposed to be, and better. My family is moving in a direction right now that if it were not for the grace of God would not be happening.

He will change our speech, change our confessions, change our profile, and change our biography. He'll change everything about us and bring us into a level of freedom we have not previously known. To be restored is to be returned to the intended purpose and use—with improvements! You may have some original parts, but God will do a new thing in and through you as well.

Reflection

I started lifting weights when I was 12 years old. My best friend and I would go from our middle school to the high school every day after school, so we could work out together. By the time we were seniors in high school, we had spent countless hours learning how to lift properly.

Every summer before our football practices began, our coaches would evaluate each player in the weight room to see if we reached a new max on our core lifts, such as the bench press, squat and power clean. The summer before our senior year, my friend and I had set a goal. We were going to break 400 pounds in the bench press—and we did! We both hit 405 pounds for a one rep max.

I will never forget how heavy that weight felt as I lifted it off the rack. I felt as though the bar could just drop to my chest and crush me. However, I managed to reach my goal along with my lifting partner and friend.

If you are not careful, you end up with either too much weight, more than you are intended to bear, or you end up with weight improperly placed resulting in injuries. I have done it myself. One day in the weight room, I dropped a 150-pound bar on my lower lip and mouth. I broke six teeth and ended up with a mouth full of stitches. I had to have three root canal procedures on my lower teeth because of the damage to the root system. The weight I dropped landed on an area that was never intended to support it, and the potential for disaster was great.

I've also seen kids drop weights and crush toes, dislocate knee caps, and knock teeth out—all of which could have been avoided if they had followed the appropriate instructions and handled the weight properly. Today, I am trained in weight lifting. I am a certified strength and conditioning coach, and I have trained countless young athletes. I have always been adamant about safety in the weight room—using proper technique and having a spotter.

But we do the same thing in life:

- We carry weights that we were never meant to carry

- We place them on areas of our lives that were never meant to bear them.

- We refuse to follow the guidance we've been given in the Word of God and end up injuring ourselves spiritually, emotionally, relationally, or even physically.

The cruel cross that Jesus bore on His back wasn't the heaviest thing He carried that day on the road to Calvary. He carried our grief and our sorrow. He carried our afflictions. He carried our transgressions by the wounds in His body. He carried our iniquities by the bruises He bore. He carried our peace through the chastisement He endured. He carried our sickness and disease through the stripes on His body (see Isaiah 53:4-5.) He carried every weight and sin that does so easily beset us (Hebrews 12:1).

The heaviest thing Jesus carried that day was the weight of all humanity. For us to stay burdened and bound is to nullify the thoroughness of His sacrifice! He bore the weight, so we do not have to bear it.

Chapter 16: Restoring Freedom

What is it that you need from God for right now? Have you sustained injury in your life? When I look back over my life, there are times when I thought I had hit bottom. I even said with my mouth, "I feel that I'm so low I have to look up to see the bottom!" He never let me even come close to the bottom. It was close enough for me, but He was still holding me up.

He is doing the same in your life right now. You may feel like you're on the bottom, weighed down by the burdens of life, but you can have this hope that God is watching over you and holding you up!

What Jesus did, He did for all. He rescued me, and He can rescue you, too. Look up, and ask Him to rescue you. Hold on for an answer, and you'll see His mighty hand coming through in your life!

David Cook

17

SEALING THE WORK

The first locust listed in Joel 1:4 is the last locust listed in Joel 2:25. The palmerworm, or gnawing locust, represents those small things, the pinhole openings that when left unaddressed can cause much more significant problems in our lives.

Philippians 1:6 says, *"And I am sure of this, that he who began a good work in you will bring it to completion at the day of Jesus Christ"* (ESV). Therefore, we cannot merely stop at having restored vision, restored reputation, and restored covering. We can't be satisfied with having the choke hold broken off our lives. God wants to make sure everything is complete. He wants to restore EVERYTHING in our lives and make sure that the cycle doesn't repeat.

My wife and I began attending a great church in our hometown in 2008. One Sunday morning, the pastor made a statement about how God will cauterize the wounds of our heart. Cauterizing a wound seals it shut and stops the loss of blood.

A wound left untreated can become infected. Infections lead to much more significant problems when left unaddressed. You could face the loss of a limb or even life due to an untreated wound. I found this to be an amazing concept when considering these small pinhole openings in our lives. We need to cover and close those areas as soon as we identify them to avoid any re-injury and infection in our spirit and our hearts.

The idea of leaving the restoration from the gnawing locust until last is significant. When restoration begins and we receive revelation from God, we get excited about the end product. In doing so, we can very quickly end up right back in the same mess again. However, as we submit ourselves to Christ, then the Spirit of the Lord will lead us into paths of righteousness. But the question still lingers—how?

When we are fully submitted, and when we have indeed learned from what we did wrong, we must set ourselves to continually seek Him to reveal areas in our lives that need to change. In all sincerity, for me this involved forgiveness.

Unforgiveness is something that everyone must deal with at some point in their Christian walk. It's a very sore spot, and it leads to other problems down the road if it is not dealt with.

Time to Move

Abraham didn't leave on his journey to the Promised Land until after his father died (Acts 7:4). We had been praying for some time about what the Lord would have us do, and how His promises to us were going to be fulfilled. I felt it was time to make a professional change, and I had been waiting on the Lord's direction. I had an idea, but I just felt it wasn't time to move yet. There was still a significant area in my life that needed to be addressed: my relationship with my father.

I went to see my father in a nursing home just south of where we live. He had received a diagnosis of cancer some months before this, and my aunt (his sister) kept me updated on his condition. He was on hospice care and was taking medication to keep him as comfortable as possible. At this point, he wasn't eating and had only received some fluids over the previous few days. His condition was deteriorating rapidly.

I felt that I needed to see him and tell him that I forgave him, and that I released him from any wrong done to me, and to apologize for harboring an offense against him. I'm grateful to have had the opportunity to do just that. He woke up for a few minutes the evening I came to visit. He looked at me, shook my hand and smiled.

I told him, "I just wanted to say that I forgive you. We are good. And I'm sorry for being angry for so long. I release you. If I do not see you again, I'll see you on the other side." It was Wednesday, October 25, 2017—the first time I had spoken to my father since 2005.

I went back to see him the next evening and sat with him for about two hours. I just talked to him about my family and my children. I told him about Joseph and that we were in the process of adopting him. I told him how God was working in our family at that time and that we were planning to return to ministry soon.

I don't know if he heard me at all, even though I've heard some say that hearing is the last thing to go. However, after that visit with him on Wednesday when we shared a brief exchange, he never woke up again. He

Chapter 17: Sealing the Work

passed away the following Sunday morning.

On Saturday, November 4, 2017, I had the privilege of speaking briefly as a part of my father's funeral service. In one part of my statement I said, "Throughout my life, the choice to have an estranged father was never mine. I do not want to rehash all that happened in my family. In the end, all that matters is that he made peace with God and secured his eternal place in Heaven through repenting of his sin and accepting Christ."

My father's funeral was a time of tremendous healing for me and for my extended family. I am grateful to the pastor who officiated at the funeral service, and who ministered to my father at the end of his life. He spoke of how my father would call him and ask that he sit with him. He said my father would often ask, "Do you think God forgives me? I've done a lot of wrongs."

During the funeral, the pastor told us how he would respond to my father when he would ask such questions. He said, "You are not a greater sinner than He is a Savior." I truly believe my father was saved and is with Jesus now. I felt the release that day which told me it was now time to move. That pinhole is sealed shut forever. Forgiveness received brings about humility. Forgiveness given brings about healing to your soul.

All the things that had happened to my father as a child—all the abuse, abandonment, and poverty, and what that produced in his life, were all washed away. The residue of his childhood had spilled over into mine, but it was all taken away.

There is power in forgiveness. Unforgiveness gives the person with whom we hold an offense power over us. Many times, that person is not even aware that we have a problem with them. They don't know, and in some cases, really do not care. Unforgiveness will keep us in bondage and leave cracks and pinholes in our lives. If there's any weakness, that is precisely where the enemy will attack.

When I released my father, something shifted in my spirit. I could feel a change coming, and there was an uprising of faith like I'd never felt before. I felt the touch of God deep in my heart. It is incredible to me to realize how deep those wounds were. God reached into my life and healed it—all of it! As far back and as deep as my family lineage reached, He restored the years of my life.

David Cook

What Consumed Me Will Sustain Me

The cry of my heart and the struggles I had endured, had produced something in me that I didn't realize was there. It created a spirit of endurance, which in turn sustains me through faith in Jesus Christ.

John the Baptist had a strong spirit of endurance. His story is recorded in all four Gospels. John's life was a fulfillment of a prophecy that came over 700 years before he burst onto the scene. Matthew's Gospel gives us a glimpse into the manner of man that John was.

The first thing we see about John is that he had a unique message. There were other preachers before John, but they preached or prophesied about things to come. John was preaching about the things that were at hand. Jesus was about to enter the scene, and John was preparing the way.

Secondly, John wore a unique garment made of camel hair. His appearance was like that of the Prophet Elijah. Elijah dressed in the same manner. A camel has tremendous endurance. They have been used to carry supplies and equipment across the deserts for centuries. Camels were also a mode of transporting people. To me, what the garment says to us about John is that he put on endurance, like a garment, and was moving people toward a new place and a new era of grace. How else could one live in the wilderness as he did?

Thirdly, John had a unique diet. Matthew says that he ate locusts and wild honey. Knowing the dietary laws of the Jewish people, one may question John's decision to consume locusts. However, the wording in Matthew implies that John was eating the actual insect, not the pod, which was allowed under the law. Nevertheless, it seems like an awful protein substitute. The honey was from wild bees and is referred to throughout the scriptures. It was also used to reference the sweetness of God's word.

God's incredible power of restoration may have already begun in our lives, but the fruit of it takes time to develop. Our voices are crying out in the wilderness, but rest assured, GOD HEARS US! He will prop us up with a spirit of endurance because of what we have battled through and because we allowed Him to do the work in our innermost being. He is going to grace us to see the work come to fruition in our lives. The restored vision, the restored ability to hear Him, the restored relationships, and the restored positioning will all happen in God's timing.

That which once consumed us will, in turn, have to sustain us. When God

Chapter 17: Sealing the Work

turns the captivity around, that which held us will be our servant. He will use the thing that bound us to deliver us, and the thing that wounded us to heal us. He will cause those devastations to become the force of strength to propel us forward into His plans and purposes. It will become our testimony! A testimony encourages us when we're down, but it also serves as a witness to others. When God seals the work in us, our lives become a testimony of deliverance, of victory, of restoration, and of hope.

It's Coming Fast

When God says in Joel 2:25, "*I will restore to you the years…*" we can count on the fact that the years we lost are going to be made up to us. Furthermore, we can count on the fact that the years we lost that were the result of the lifestyles our parents chose, or their parents chose, are coming back to us. It will be as though time compresses, and God will do more with less time than we thought imaginable. When God restores the years we lost while living in sin, it is as if He propels and accelerates us into our destiny.

Amos 9:13 in The Message Bible is of particular interest concerning the speed with which God will move:

"Yes indeed, it won't be long now." GOD's Decree. "Things are going to happen so fast your head will swim, one thing fast on the heels of the other. You won't be able to keep up. Everything will be happening at once—and everywhere you look, blessings! Blessings like wine pouring off the mountains and hills. I'll make everything right again for my people Israel."

In this passage, he speaks of restoration happening so fast our heads will spin. It may seem like a sudden rush, like in Acts 2 when the Holy Spirit fell on the 120 in the Upper Room. He came suddenly, like a mighty rushing wind and fell on all of them and they were all filled with the Holy Spirit. Of course, we know that in Acts 2, they had been praying for ten days. In Amos 9, there were years of bondage that God was going to overthrow. But when He begins to move, He can compress time and cause things to accelerate to get us where He desires for us to be.

Joel 2:23 says that God will cause the former and the latter rain to fall together in the same month. If we endure, if we want to give up on God altogether and don't, God will bring us out. The spirit of endurance is upon us, and that which attacked us will now have to sustain us.

Reflection

After my father passed away, I was speaking with a friend of ours in our ministerial organization. As I shared a little bit of my history with my father, my friend hugged me and said, "I'd like to pray with you." This man knows us, and he knows our hearts. As he prayed with me, he said, "Just as you waited to move Abraham until after his father died, let this be done. Move my brother quickly into that which you have called him to."

Since that time, we have moved at a steady pace. We are positioning ourselves in every possible way. God has shifted things in our home, our work, our family, our schedules—all so we can pursue His calling on our lives.

There is a time to move. Sometimes, though, we have to wait for the work that is happening in us to be to a point where we can advance. Our voice may be as one crying out for help. We may be consuming a diet that is less than desirable. Hold on! The pinhole is closing, and God is sealing the work in us. Rest assured, if He began the good work, He will see to it that it's complete!

18

A SPIRIT OF ADOPTION

I remember lining up in gym class or at recess at school and waiting hopefully while two children would pick teams for kickball, basketball, or whatever game we were playing that day. I can't recall a time when I got to be the one picking. I was usually one of the last ones chosen for the team. I wasn't an outstanding athlete. I couldn't run very fast, and I was somewhat uncoordinated.

We moved around a lot, so my classmates didn't know me all that well. It wasn't until I got to high school, and worked hard at it, that I was even able to put on a uniform.

Early on, I realized that the choosing of teams was more of a social thing than it was about athletics. The "captains" tended to pick their friends first. Since I wasn't friends with them, I didn't get chosen. Now, this has not caused some deep emotional wound, nor do I have a broken psyche over it. I'm sure when I was a kid that had some impact on me. I'm sure I went home sad a few times, but I don't remember anything specific.

What I did learn from this was that if I didn't want to be last, I needed to connect with the right people. I didn't want to be last nor did I want to be at the bottom. This mindset indeed carried over into adulthood. For several years, I tried and tried to make connections.

However, when God called me out, when He saved me, He picked me! God does not look for the most qualified or the most talented. He looks for the willing. It doesn't matter that I was broken before. It doesn't matter that I do not have the right pedigree. It doesn't matter to God whether or not I can throw a baseball or make a basket from the three-point line. God is not concerned with my charisma or my connections. He is looking for my contrition before Him.

Those kids on the playgrounds and in gym classes yelling, "Pick me! Pick me," appear to be going about it all wrong in God's eyes. He's not necessarily looking for the one who will scream for attention but rather for the one who will exalt Him. My struggles in life serve to glorify God.

Paul said in 2 Corinthians 12:9, *"Most gladly therefore will I rather glory in my infirmities, that the power of Christ may rest upon me."* His strength is made perfect in my weakness. My testimony then is about how amazing His grace is. What we face in life then serves two purposes: first, to draw us closer to the Savior; second, to help someone else that they might be saved.

Using What I Know

God will often use what we know. In Matthew 17, the disciples came with Jesus into Capernaum. The collectors of the temple tax asked Peter, "Does your teacher not pay the tax?" (v. 24, ESV).

Jesus then turned to Peter and said, "What do you think, Simon?" (v. 25, ESV).

Jesus said, "However, not to give offense to them, go to the sea and cast a hook and take the first fish that comes up, and when you open its mouth you will find a shekel. Take that and give it to them for me and for yourself" (v. 27, ESV).

In this case, Jesus took what Peter knew how to do, something he was exposed to in his past, and used it to meet a need. The shekel found in the fish's mouth was enough to pay the tax and then some. Furthermore, the fish was good for food. So not only did Jesus meet the financial need, but He provided for a physical need as well. The answer was in the mouth of the fish—in the thing that Peter understood how to do.

At times in life, we tend to go back to what we know. We grow tired, frustrated, and weary in well doing, so we revert to responses we know all too well. In John 21, Peter appeared to be frustrated and said, "I'm going fishing" (John 21:3, ESV). The Bible says that the others went with him, even though not all of them were fishermen. They toiled all night, in something that was a part of their life before encountering Jesus, and caught nothing. Peter knew how to fish; he knew where the fish were. It was his career and his area of expertise.

Jesus was there on the shore at daybreak and told them to cast their nets on the other side. They did, and they were not able to get all the fish into the boat.

In this one moment, Jesus gave him an idea of what his ministry would be. Peter was a fisherman, but Jesus called him to be a fisher of men. In Acts 2, Peter preached the first sermon of the infant church, and 3,000 souls came to

Chapter 18: A Spirit of Adoption

Jesus that day. The catch of souls was great. God had used what Peter knew to teach him how to do it.

I knew what it was like to be fatherless. I understood, at least to some degree, what it was like to be rejected, and subsequently, to reject others. Some people have faced much worse, but this sort of wounds in your heart is not something to be glossed over. It takes a lot of grace, love, and forgiveness to get past it. I wasn't an orphan in the sense that I had no family. However, I can relate to the feeling of rejection, since I knew that my father didn't want me.

A few years ago, I worked in a boarding school for troubled teens. Several of the boys I worked with were adopted. They struggled with the notion that their natural parents didn't want them. I recall one young man telling me he couldn't see how his mother and father could give him up and walk away, with no regard for what happened to him. One afternoon, he got into some trouble, and we were talking about the family that had adopted him. I'll never forget this. He said, "Yeah, they adopted me, but they have their kids. They don't want me. I'm nothing but trouble for them. No one wants me."

There were at least a few young men like this in that school. I prayed about what the Lord would have me say to them, and He showed me. We see throughout the Bible that the nation of Israel is God's chosen people. Those who are descendants of Abraham are born into that covenant, by blood, because of God's promises to Abraham. However, those of us who have accepted God's free gift of salvation through Christ are also chosen.

The Bible says it is the will of God that everyone should be saved (1 Timothy 2:4), but we know that not all will accept it. Scripture also tells us that we can't get saved whenever we want to because it is the Holy Spirit who leads us to repentance, and subsequently to salvation (Romans 2:4). In that sense, we are chosen!

An adopted child, then, is one that the parents decide to add to their family. Natural children are born into families without the luxury of choice. God has given us as humans the ability to procreate, and we are commanded to do so, and we love and nurture our children. However, when families decide to adopt, they are uniquely preaching the Gospel.

Meeting Myself in Joseph

In 2016, there were 437,000 children nationwide in foster care, according to the US Department of Health and Human Services. Of that number, 118,000 were waiting to be adopted. These numbers have steadily increased since 2012. I have worked in public education for several years now. The needs that children are facing today—living in fatherless and, in some cases, parentless homes—is just staggering to me. When I was a child, only a few of my classmates lived in single-parent homes. Most of my friends' parents were married—and are still married today.

My wife and I had the heart to do something, but, at first, we were not sure what that "something" was. That "something" soon became clear: making Joseph a member of our family. Joseph has become such a big piece of what the Lord is doing in our lives and family that I want to tell a bit more of his story.

In the spring of 2015, my wife and I embarked on a journey we had never been through before. Several years earlier, we had discussed becoming foster parents, or possibly adopting another child. However, it was now 2015. I had two children out of high school, and the third was a junior. We were about to be out of the parenting business. I never thought we would follow through on this, especially at this point in our lives.

At the time we met Joseph, Becca was working in the Early Childhood Center in our school district as an aide. She worked in Joseph's class, and he just latched on to her. My youngest daughter would go over to that class to do some volunteer tutoring hours for the Missouri A+ Program. She would come home talking about Joseph almost every day. Joseph was living with his great-grandparents—and had been for the majority of his young life. They were hoping to find a family willing to help out and possibly adopt Joseph, so his future could be assured. At that time, Joseph had just turned five years old.

I can tell you with all sincerity that I was not in favor of this at first. I was afraid to try it for my own sake, and for Joseph's. I didn't want to grow attached to this little boy and then have it fall through. Our oldest son, Nick, was in college at the time we started this. Our middle daughter, Sarah, was also in college. Our youngest, Ashley, was a junior in high school and was planning to go to college in the fall of 2016. Furthermore, I didn't do such an excellent job of being there for them, and I was worried I might blow this even worse.

My opposition also included a bit of a selfish motive. We were about to be out of the child-raising phase of our lives, and I didn't want to run headlong back into the parenting gig. I felt like our marriage was beginning to stabilize, and I didn't want to disrupt that and run the risk of making it worse than before.

However, by the end of March 2015, God apprehended my heart, and I felt such peace about it. Becca and I talked it over, and what it would mean for our family and us. It was no secret to either of us that we were trying to stabilize our home in every possible way. Our marriage had been rocky for several years, and our financial house was still reeling from a bankruptcy. But we felt that God had brought Joseph to us, and we decided to look into what it would take to make it happen.

We talked to our children, who all added a resounding "Yes!" We spoke with our pastors. They prayed with us and supported us in moving toward adopting Joseph. After that, we decided to talk to Joseph's great-grandparents.

Becca spoke with her boss, the person at the school who had told her that Joseph's great-grandparents were looking for a permanent placement for him. We told her we'd like to talk to them about adopting him. The meeting was arranged, and Joseph's teacher, the building director, Joseph's great-grandparents, Becca and I all met to discuss the future of this little boy.

After the meeting, we agreed to take some steps to get to know Joseph. We would allow him to meet the rest of our family and see what our lifestyle was like. We would then reconvene to decide on a path forward.

We talked to our extended family, all of whom responded with support. We accepted all of this as God's "Amen!" to this step of faith.

The very first day we spent some time with Joseph was for an Easter Egg Hunt in the park in March 2015. We took him to the hunt, along with his great-grandfather, and then took him out to lunch. He did so good and seemed to have a great time. When I dropped Joseph off at his great-grandparents house that afternoon, he stood in the doorway crying, not wanting us to leave. Joseph's fear of people leaving him was a common problem for him for some time after. He didn't want to leave the house with us, but he didn't want us to leave him there, either. The same was true when his great-grandparents brought him to our house. He didn't want them to leave, but he didn't want to leave us.

Having dealt with children who suffered from Reactive Attachment Disorder, I began to think that maybe that was what was going on with Joseph.

This condition comes about from children having an extreme lack of parental contact as babies. It may seem elementary, but holding them, feeding them, rocking them to sleep, playing with them, smiling and laughing with them, and reading to them, all play a part in a child's development. Joseph seemed gripped with the fear that we all may leave him and never return.

Over the next several months, he spent afternoons with us after school and accompanied my wife to track meets while I was coaching in the spring. Eventually, we shifted everyone around to different bedrooms, and he began spending the night at our house through the week and going to his great-grandparents on the weekend. They even started attending our church with Joseph. They came every single Sunday.

The more time I spent with Joseph, the more I saw myself. His natural father never had anything to do with him. The man had only seen Joseph a few times. At one point, he denied that Joseph was even his son. Joseph's natural mother would take him to her grandparent's home and run off, leaving him there.

At one point, she was in a hospital for mental health reasons and said to a nurse, "I don't think I can handle that kid. I'm going to hurt him." We later learned that she would often leave him to cry alone in his room, with the door locked so he couldn't get out. Other times, she would leave for days or weeks at a time.

When I looked at him, I saw so many similarities with my own life. I saw a boy with no father. I saw a boy whose father denied him. In my case, my dad told me many times I was not his son and that he disowned me. I saw a boy who had someone who was not his parent trying to care for him. In my case, my grandmother lived with me until I was 15 and helped care for me while my mother worked. In Joseph's case, he was left alone with his great-grandparents.

Joseph was shunned by even some members of his own family because of something he couldn't control: his race. Joseph is biracial. I felt shunned my entire childhood because of something I couldn't control: my father's bizarre behaviors. In Joseph, I saw a child who had a minimal chance in life. His great-grandparents loved him, there was no doubt about that, but they knew they couldn't care for him to adulthood. In so many ways, when I look at Joseph, I see myself. I see a broken boy who needed a father, and I was determined to do for him what my father could not do for me, and in doing so, continue to

Chapter 18: A Spirit of Adoption

repair my relationships with my own children and in my home.

Reflection

Most of my life, I've longed to be a son. Many of the issues I faced in my life can be linked to a desire to be validated as a son. There is something lost in life when we don't have that link with other people. We need the relationships and support of peers, but we also need the love, accountability, and validation provided by those older than us, such as our parents. If we've missed out on that part, it can be difficult to overcome.

From the time Joseph started staying with us in the summer months of 2015 until now, we have seen tremendous improvements in his behavior at home and social settings, such as church and school. One thing we noticed around mid-summer in 2016, Joseph started going to bed on his own much more easily than before. When he first started staying with us, one of us would have to hold him until he fell fast asleep and was snoring. Joseph gets warm and sweats a lot, and we'd have to take a shower after he went to bed!

He wouldn't go into his room. He was terrified, and would say over and over, "It's not going to get me. He's not going to be scared."

I started telling him every night, "Joseph, nothing is going to get you, because I have got you! Always! As long as you're with me, I will not let anything happen to you!" At night now, I ask him, "You don't have to be scared, do you know why?"

He responds, "Yes, because Coach (or Dad) *gots* me."

Joseph was insecure and afraid of being alone, and his behavior sometimes showed it. We have been able to provide the security he so desperately needed. When I look at Joseph, I see myself when I was young. I was insecure, afraid and, at times, just plain terrified of being alone.

Even into my adult life, I battled that same thing. God is using that to bring peace to Joseph every single day. We see victories with him on a continual basis. God is doing a miraculous thing in his life, and I'm so honored to be a part of it!

Romans 8:15 says, *"For you did not receive the spirit of slavery to fall back into fear, but you have received the Spirit of adoption as sons, by whom we cry, 'Abba! Father!'"* (ESV). Regardless then of our heritage or our lineage, if we're saved, we are validated as a son or a daughter in God's house. God has adopted us adopted into His family.

The next few verses tell us that we are heirs and joint heirs with Jesus. In other words, if Jesus is the King and receives the King's inheritance from the Father, then we obtain that same inheritance through Christ. Fatherless, motherless, friendless—it doesn't matter! If we're in Him, we are not alone. We are adopted! Those whom the Lord calls out, He also validates. Our identity in Christ becomes our validation in life!

19

PROGRESSING IN FAITH

We found an attorney to represent us in our adoption case for a nominal fee, compared to what I thought it would cost. We met with him in May 2015. After our second meeting, we agreed to retain him as our attorney. When we met with him to prepare our official filing with the court, he handed me an invoice. I slipped it into the red folder we called "The Joseph File."

"Did you happen to look at your invoice?" he asked us as we were leaving. I told him that neither of us had just yet, but we trusted what he had quoted us. He said, "You may want to look at it. I'm pretty sure I only charged you half of what I quoted you over the phone. I will honor it, but I think I gave you a pretty good deal."

When we got home, we saw that he had charged us EXACTLY half of what he quoted. I thought the original amount was very fair, so this was a blessing!

Over all, our costs were significantly less than I anticipated. We incurred costs including the initial bill from our attorney, court filing fees, background checks, items needed for our home to pass the inspection performed during the home study, and for the home study itself. It all cost a FRACTION of what private adoptions typically cost. I said to my wife numerous times, "There is no way that's all this will cost."

As we finished the preliminary work with the home study, meeting with the attorney, and preparing our case for court, we were met with literally no opposition. Once our attorney filed our case, Joseph was assigned a Guardian Ad Litem, someone who would represent the best interests of the child in court. It so happened that the attorney who was appointed to be the Guardian Ad Litem was the same attorney who had represented Joseph when he was placed with his great-grandparents two years before, so she had a history with his case.

Roadblocks

We met with the Guardian Ad Litem, and she seemed to be in favor of Joseph coming to live with us permanently. With her agreement, the case appeared to be a lock. So, the first court date was set for August 10, 2015. At a minimum, we were to assume guardianship of Joseph that day. No one had heard from either of the natural parents, so we were not sure they would even show up.

When we arrived at the courthouse that day with our attorney and Joseph's great-grandparents, there stood Joseph's natural father. He had read the posting of the case in the county's legal publication and had decided to contest the adoption and try to get custody. This man had never visited, supported, called, inquired, or done anything for Joseph. In fact, for some time after Joseph was born, he had denied that he was the natural father.

The judge ordered an attorney to be appointed to represent the father. The case was continued until November, and for the next two and a half years, we were in a battle to adopt Joseph. The natural mother did not show up initially, although she did about a year later.

When Joseph was born, she had been living with her grandparents (Joseph's great-grandparents) and had left Joseph there multiple times. The last time, she told a medical professional, "I can't care for him. I'm afraid I'll hurt him." So that began the shift when he was placed with the great-grandparents permanently. Eventually, the natural father and the natural mother both received court-appointed counsel.

We never made it to the November court date. In October, we were called back to court because the attorney for the natural father had filed a motion for visitation rights for his client, and to attempt to collect his legal fees from us. Believe it or not, there is precedent for this. We could have been ordered by the court to pay the fees for the court-appointed representation of the father, since he could not afford to pay it himself. Thanks to the testimony of the Guardian Ad Litem, and the rebuttal by our attorney on the fees, the judge did not grant either motion. Our hearing was continued again until December.

Between the time we went to court in October until the time of our new court date in December, our case was assigned to a different judge. There had been an election, and some of the judges were shifting around. We were then given another continuance and another date in February for the case to be heard. Then we were continued until April, and then June, and on and on. This cycle went on for the next year and a half. In all, we had eight continuances, mostly due to changes in legal counsel for the natural parents.

The natural father had at least six different attorneys over the course of that two-and-a-half-year period, and the natural mother had two.

Behavior Explained

From the time we first met Joseph, we knew something was different about him. He had challenges with things that "normal-functioning" kids his age did not. He seemed to have a fantastic memory and capacity for visual recognition, but he lagged in social cues and certain academic areas. He struggled with going to the bathroom, going to bed, getting up in the morning, or coming to the table for dinner. Granted, he was getting ready to go into kindergarten, but he was not at grade level in many things.

In July 2016, we received a diagnosis for Joseph. He had some definitive challenges from a behavioral perspective, and we needed to find out what was going on. It appeared to be a neurological condition of some kind, but we had to find out what it was, so that he could receive the help he needed. We had some evaluations completed and learned that Joseph's diagnosis was Level 2 Autism Spectrum Disorder. This fueled our desire to complete this process all the more. We realized that he needed support and help, and we had to have guardianship, at a minimum, to make it happen.

In November 2016, Joseph came down with pneumonia. He had to be hospitalized for a week, and he missed nearly three weeks of school. During this time, his great-grandfather and Becca took care of him. Being so ill was difficult for Joseph, because he couldn't communicate how he was feeling, what hurt, or what he wanted. It was such a trying time for him and our family.

Change Is in the Air

As we entered 2017, God was at work in our lives. We were reconnecting with people we knew in ministry. My middle daughter had decided to attend the same Bible college I had attended, and I agreed to take her for a visit in April, which would be the first time I had been on the campus of the church since 2003.

However, we still felt like we were not any closer to realizing our goal of adoption. We faced multiple continuances throughout the next few months. We finally had the opportunity for a guardianship transfer on May 19, 2017. Our attorney felt that if we could get this done, then the court would have to, according to Missouri statute, hear our petition for adoption in six months.

We were granted the guardianship on May 19, and at that time, only the natural father came to court. Both attorneys representing the natural parents stated that their clients consented to guardianship, but would not agree to the subsequent adoption. Mainly, we were going to have to submit evidence proving *abandonment* when we came back to court. Our entire case for adoption hinged on our attorney's ability to show this. November 30, 2017 was set as the date for the adoption hearing.

Abandonment under Missouri statute occurs when there is no contact or monetary support of any kind given to the minor child for six months before the filing of the adoption. We had the great-grandfather's testimony which proved that. Neither parent had done anything for Joseph from at least as far back as December 2014. Therefore, our claim of *abandonment* was legitimate.

Over the course of the two years leading up to the May 19 court date, Joseph's great-grandmother had developed some significant health issues, and she took a definitive turn for the worse throughout 2017. She had one leg amputated below the knee, due to complications related to diabetes. She was in and out of the hospital, and she even stayed in a nursing home for some time. She had finally returned home in July.

On Saturday morning, July 15, 2017, Becca and I were out to breakfast. Joseph had gone over to his great-grandparents house for the weekend, as he still does a couple of times each month. We received a call from Joseph's great-grandfather just before the waitress brought our order to us. Joseph wanted to come home. He was behaving well and had not had any accidents related to the bathroom. He just wanted to come home. While we were on the phone with Joseph's great-grandfather, his son came into the room and said, "Dad, I think mom passed away."

We later found out that Joseph had tried to wake her up earlier that morning and she wouldn't wake up, so he said he wanted to come home. We all knew that she wanted nothing more than to see Joseph placed in a good home with parents who would care for him. Thankfully, she knew that we received guardianship before she passed away.

From the time Joseph started staying with us through the week and going to his great-grandparents on the weekends, his great-grandparents had been coming to church with us. They both stated that they enjoyed the church very much and planned to continue coming to support Joseph and us. His great-grandfather continued attending even after his wife died.

Reflection

God's ultimate plan for us is that of redemption. The story of salvation, at least to me, is so evident in the process of adoption. Here was a little boy who didn't know why no one cared, he just knew that the people who should, didn't. He was behaving in ways that were natural to him because he didn't have any frame of reference for anything else. He was lost.

And so were we before Christ found us. Regardless of what we've done, God still loves us and cares for us. It's not too late, and we are not too far gone that He will refuse us. The fact that you're reading this now is proof that God is still passionately pursuing you! He loves you with such abandon that He gave all He had to save you!

David Cook

20

TIME TO TESTIFY

I grew up going to church. We attended some very conservative, denominational churches. Sunday was a full day, with Sunday school starting at 9:00 a.m., morning worship starting at 10:00 a.m. and lasting until at least noon, and other events often starting as early as 5:00 p.m. We were always there for the evening service which started at 7:00 p.m. and often lasted two hours, sometimes longer. Most of the families who brought children to Sunday evening services would allow them to lay down on the pew or under it. We still went to school on Monday morning.

We had our mid-week service and youth group meetings on Wednesday night. On top of that, we had periodic revival meetings which always lasted two hours or more and were often scheduled for several nights in a row.

One of the mainstays of Sunday night services was what we called a "testimony service." If you've ever been in such a service, you'll know what I'm talking about. The churches we attended practiced what I would call "popcorn" testimonies.

The pastor would stand up and say, "Does anyone have a testimony they'd like to share?" This call for a testimony was followed by what seemed to be an eternity of awkward silence until one brave saint would pop up and give a testimony.

Most of the time, the testimony ended with this phrase, "Just pray for me that I'll go all the way with Him." After the first person spoke, others would begin to stand and share their testimonies as well.

Now, I'm not making fun of this. These people loved God. Most of them were genuine in their desire to encourage others, and brag about the goodness of Jesus in their lives. Of course, we had some flakey ones, but not any more than we do today. The important factor here is that a testimony has power!

Revelation 12:11 says we overcome by the blood of the Lamb and the word of our testimony. Therefore, it's important to write it down, share it, speak it, and remind God of it on a regular basis.

Before David squared off against Goliath, he said, "*The LORD who delivered me from the paw of the lion and from the paw of the bear will deliver me from the hand of this Philistine*" (1 Samuel 17:37, ESV). After this testimony, Saul told David to go ahead and face Goliath. I would argue that Goliath was defeated the moment David shared his testimony, because of the confidence and faith that arose in David's heart.

So, if you'll excuse me for just a minute, I want to testify about how the restoration of God has been at work in our lives on so many levels, bringing us back to the place from which we started.

Back to the Beginning

As I think back to that early morning on August 5, 2017, standing there in a hotel room preparing to preach for the first time in 14 years, I cannot comprehend with my natural mind how God could ever love me, much less consider me worthy of such a holy assignment.

Our lives are beginning to circle back to the beginning, and this time the path is much different and much clearer. Like that restored classic car, God is restoring us to our intended use and purpose.

When you drive past a construction site before the work begins, it may appear to be an absolute mess. There is equipment everywhere, and materials are strewn all over the site. Before you can see anything that resembles a building, you'll notice that the ground and the natural environment must be disturbed to get them to a place where the foundation can be laid or poured. This process may take weeks or sometimes months.

Before the building can take shape, plans have to be drawn up. There are usually several versions of the blueprints before any work begins. Permits must be obtained to build the structure legally, and surveys must be completed to know precisely where to start building.

Everything about that new building must be addressed. Where will the doors and windows be? How will people enter the building? Where will they park? How many restrooms will there be, and where will they be positioned? And don't forget heating, cooling, and ventilation. Most importantly, the architect and their team must consider the overall size and weight of the structure, to ensure they use the proper materials rated to handle the intended design and use of the facility.

Chapter 20: Time to Testify

To those of us who are not directly involved in the planning or the unseen work that goes into a building, we might casually pass by and ponder, "I wonder what that will be?"

But when the foundation is in place, and that building comes up out of the ground, then we take notice. It no longer looks like a pile of materials and storage lot for heavy equipment and machinery. It is beginning to look like what that architect envisioned when he drew the plans. To the casual observer, the building appeared to take shape at a rapid pace, but few understand the months—and sometimes years—of planning that went into getting the structure to that point.

I can't speak for everyone, but this is what God is doing in my life. I was sharing this story with a pastor I know, and he said, "Man, we didn't know. You masked it so well. I don't know if anyone around here ever picked up on what was going on with you guys. But look at you now!"

Then I told him, "Restoration, when it becomes visible, will always appear to be rapid to the casual observer. But like that new building, no one understands the months and years of process it took to get to a *suddenly* moment."

In looking back to the beginning of this journey I've shared, there were fourteen years of struggle, of bitterness, of trying everything I could try to appease the gnawing in my soul to get to the point where I was willing to listen to God. I asked God to change me radically. I asked Him to make me despise what He despises, and to love what He loves. As God promised in Ezekiel 36:26, I asked Him to give me a new heart of flesh, because mine was cold and brittle. God answered my prayer.

From 2014 until 2017, I prayed like the sinner in Luke 18:13. I stayed in the background at church. I stayed in the background at home. I did not feel worthy to take the lead as the priest of my house. I hated what my life had become, and I hated the fact that I had shunned my responsibilities as a husband and father and walked away from my calling. In 2017, something turned. God began to infuse me with a new boldness in prayer and faith.

Time Is Accelerating

In the summer of 2017, time seemed to accelerate. We decided we were going to explore some avenues of returning to ministry. We met with our pastors and talked with other people we knew in ministry and asked for input and advice. In July of 2017, we took a trip to Ohio to attend the camp meeting held by the organization I'm credentialed through. We had not been to the camp meeting since 2003, and it was like a homecoming for us—we had an excellent time!

Just before we left to go to Ohio, I had a dream. In my dream, I saw the pastor of the church walking toward us. He stopped, hugged us, then nudged my shoulder, and said, "Where have you been?"

I responded, "I've been hiding because I failed, and I was ashamed."

He responded, "Well, you're back now. Let's get back to work!" And he walked off.

The second day of the conference, there was a meeting for all members of the ministry organization. They had just reinstated my ordination one month prior, so we attended. At the meeting, the pastor rolled out the vision for a brand-new ministry network.

During this meeting, the events from my dream transpired almost exactly the way they happened in the dream. We were greatly encouraged in our desire to return to ministry, and God has been moving in such a fantastic way for us since.

I've laughed at this often, because I had said, "I'll not go back. That part of my life is over."

BUT GOD said, "If you'll submit to Me, I'll take you back to where you once believed!" God has restored so much in our lives, and I cannot begin to thank Him enough. Having the opportunity to go back to what I consider to be my home church again, and to be received as we were by so many beautiful people, has been nothing short of amazing to me. I know what manner of man I am, and God still sees fit to use me in His service. I'm so grateful for all that God is doing for us by reconnecting us to our covering. We go there about every six weeks now, and it has been just a fantastic return home.

He WILL Provide

Around the beginning of June, we received a somewhat unexpected bill from our attorney. Because the adoption case went on for so long, and because the natural parents were trying to fight us, we were going to have to come up with more money.

Because of the nature of her job, my wife doesn't receive a paycheck two

Chapter 20: Time to Testify

months out of the year. The attorney's bill was due right in the middle of one of those months.

I took on a second job and worked all summer painting, while still holding down my regular position as the head football coach at our school. Anyone who knows anything about coaching, particularly football, knows that the summer is not a vacation—it's the pre-season. I found myself working non-stop, but I was committed to seeing the adoption through to completion.

We were leading a small group in our home during the summer months of 2017. One night in mid-June, just before our group meeting started, another car pulled up into our driveway. It was a former football player whom I had coached who was just stopping by to say hello.

During our conversation, it seemed like he wanted to tell me something. All of a sudden, tears welled up in his eyes, and he reached into his pocket and pulled out some money. He said, "Here. Take this. It's for Joseph. You did so much to help me, and I want Joseph to have the benefit of having you and Miss Becca as his parents."

I was speechless. After he left, I went back into the house for our small group meeting. I couldn't tell you what our video was about that night because I was in shock because of what had just happened. As I sat down in the chair after the video started, I heard the Lord say, "You will not need to fight this battle. I will fight it for you. I will provide for you. I can cause ravens to feed you if necessary. Stand still and see."

From that moment until we went to court in November, people just began to hand us money to help with the adoption. It wasn't much money in the grand scheme of things, but it was enough. With Becca not receiving a paycheck that month, and with the other things we had in front of us, coming up with the money to pay the attorney's bill had seemed unreachable. But God provided! And, at the same time, our overall giving increased.

Everything Is Ready—Now the Answer Can Come

We finally went to court for the adoption case on November 30, 2017. The natural mother never showed up that day. There was some concern that she may have been in the hospital. If so, that would have delayed the case even more. The judge gave her attorney three weeks to investigate, and we were slated to reconvene on December 20, 2017. I was frustrated, and I wondered just how much longer this could take. But the judge that day stated, "We *will* hear this case by the end of the year. It's gone on long enough."

During the proceedings on November 30, 2017, something else came up while the court was on the record: who was paying the Guardian Ad Litem's fees for her work on the case? When the judge asked, "Are the Cooks paying your legal fees?" I felt like time stopped! My heart sank, and fear gripped me. I leaned over to Becca and whispered, "Oh, God help us! We can't afford to pay her. How much could it be? We don't have it! What are we going to do?"

The Guardian Ad Litem told the judge, "Oh, I decided to waive my fee. I represented Joseph when he was placed with the great-grandparents five years ago, and I received compensation through the county at that time. I decided to waive the fee for this case to see to it that Joseph had a permanent placement."

Our sigh of relief must have been noticeable in the courtroom. When we got back to our car that afternoon, we looked at each other in amazement! God had provided AGAIN!

We went back to court Wednesday, December 20, 2017, at 1:00 p.m. As I walked off the elevator that morning, I prayed and said, "Lord, back in June, You told me I would not have to fight this battle. Fight for Joseph today."

There was a restroom on the same floor as our courtroom. I was feeling a bit anxious about the case, and I wanted to go in and wash my face with cold water. The restroom was private, and the moment I walked in and locked the door, I turned around and saw a mountain. On that mountain was the face of opposition. As I looked at that mountain in front of me, all of a sudden, I said, "Mountain, MOVE!", and the mountain was gone.

A few minutes after I came out of the restroom, our attorney came to us and told us that the natural father was no longer going to contest the adoption, but he was not going to consent. Mostly, he was saying that this was a done deal, aside from the formality of actually receiving a ruling from the judge. After waiting around in the hallway for over an hour, we finally went into the courtroom. The natural mother didn't show up again. Her attorney reported she was not in the hospital, and although he had made multiple attempts to contact her, she had not returned any of his calls. He requested to be relieved from the case, which he was. The natural father's attorney stated on the record that they were no longer going to contest the adoption, but they were not going to consent to it, either. That meant, for the most part, all our attorney had to do

Chapter 20: Time to Testify

was present the evidence in the case, proving our claim of abandonment of the child.

There is power in testimony! We overcome by the blood of the Lamb and the word of our testimony. Joseph's great-grandfather was called to the witness stand first, and the attorney's line of questioning presented evidence related to the fact that no contact or attempted contact by either of the natural parents had occurred for six months prior to the filing of the adoption, or since.

Following Joseph's great-grandfather, our attorney called me to the witness stand. The line of questioning for me mainly centered around the current state of our home, family, and employment. I was asked to testify as to Joseph's wellbeing and his current diagnosis of Autism Spectrum Disorder.

My wife was called next, and her testimony was merely to corroborate my statement. Our testimony primarily involved answering a few *yes* or *no* questions about information the court already had. Our attorney and the Guardian Ad Litem only questioned the three of us. The natural father's attorney never cross-examined us, nor did the judge present any other questions or call for additional information.

After all of the testimony was in, the judge asked if any of the attorneys present in court that day had any other statements to add while we were still on record. At this time, the Guardian Ad Litem spoke up and said, "I was the original Guardian Ad Litem on Joseph's case in 2013 when his great-grandparents were awarded guardianship. I chose to waive my fee to see this through to completion so that Joseph could be placed in a permanent home. Having met with the Cooks and seeing them with Joseph several times over the past two and half years, I believe it would be to the child's detriment to remove him from their care. I am in full support of the adoption of the child by this family."

At 2:45 p.m. on December 20, 2017, after being assigned to three different judges, after eight continuances of our hearing, and after 933 days of waiting, hoping, and praying, our petition for the adoption of Joseph was finalized, along with our request to legally change his last name to ours.

On that day, a mountain MOVED out of our way, and God gave us tremendous favor! The Lord made a way, and we did not have to fight this battle at all. I looked at Becca after the judge issued her ruling in our favor, and said, "That's it? No more court dates? Don't we have to do or say something else?" It was finally over, and Joseph was permanently placed in our family.

In Joel 2:25, God says, "*I will restore to you the years....*" When God does that, He will even restore things you didn't lose. We didn't lose Joseph. But God knew that he needed a family, and that we needed him. God knew that when I looked at Joseph, I would see myself in so many ways. He used what I knew—I could understand rejection, abandonment, and fatherlessness. God will use what you know, and He will take what consumed you and force it to sustain you. Therefore, out of our struggle, God produced a miracle to help the helpless!

Mother Teresa once said, "If you can't feed a hundred people, then feed just one." My wife and I have a heart for our city, for our community, and for the nations. However, if we're not willing to feed one, reach one, help one, or minister to one, how can we ever expect to do the same for multitudes? We decided that Joseph would be our start, our *one*. And God is blessing that!

Reflection

As I pondered a more focused and intimate relationship with God after our adoption was final, the Holy Spirit spoke to my heart, and said, "You are most susceptible to attack following your greatest victory." Too often, we will take time off from our routines following a breakthrough or victory, thinking that we can rest now. We are most vulnerable following our most significant wins.

By all means, we must celebrate wins. We must recount the blessings and tell the stories. Testifying of the goodness of God is key. That is why I wrote this book: to tell the story of how God restored my family, my ministry, and most importantly, my salvation.

We cannot neglect our spiritual growth. I love to tell the story about how the Lord moved in our lives, but I realize that I need to continue to grow and seek God. I have to put the old man down and continually put on the new nature of Christ. I can't rest in yesterday's place of victory, I need to keep pressing *"...toward the mark for the prize of the high calling of God in Christ Jesus"* (Philippians 3:14).

Joel 2:26-27 describes the post-restoration life:

And ye shall eat in plenty, and be satisfied, and praise the name of the LORD *your God, that hath dealt wondrously with you: and my people shall* ***never*** *be ashamed. And* *ye shall know that I am in the midst of Israel, and that I am the* LORD *your God, and none else: and my people shall never be ashamed.*

As we read on through the end of the chapter, God promises an outpouring of His Spirit on all people. There is a humility that comes from being broken. There is a willingness to attribute proper credit to the appropriate source after we have walked through a season of dryness, bitterness and shame. When we get to the point where we are rending our hearts before God, and we are offering the sacrifice of tears before Him, there is a profound work that takes place in our innermost being.

Psalm 34:19 says, *"Many are the afflictions of the righteous: but the Lord delivereth him out of them all."* Notice, the Psalmist says *all*, not *some*. He doesn't put conditions on it. He says God will deliver us out of them ALL!

I should have been poor...BUT God provided for me!
I should have been addicted...BUT God delivered me!
I should have been sick...BUT God healed me!
I should have been divorced...BUT God intervened for me!
I should have been alone...BUT God never left me!

The devil had me down, BUT God delivered me from his snare! God, through the power of the Holy Spirit, transitioned me from a place of failure and defeat into a position of recovery and restoration. Jesus Himself is our example of victory. When He walked out of the tomb on that very first Easter morning, death and defeat were still trying to figure out how He slipped through their fingers, for His body was no longer in the grave.

We have that same nature, that same spirit that raised Christ from the dead dwelling in us. We have been raised in newness of life with Him, and the enemy is powerless against the finished work of Christ.

I'm so glad that the Lord restored me. Thanks be to God forever! My prayer is that you will encounter that same Spirit of victory, and that your restoration begins even today. In Jesus' Name, AMEN!

David Cook

David Cook is available for book interviews and personal appearances. For more information contact:

David Cook
C/O Advantage Books
P.O. Box 160847
Altamonte Springs, FL 32716
info@advbooks.com

To purchase additional copies of this book visit our bookstore website at:
www.advbookstore.com

Longwood, Florida, USA
"we bring dreams to life"™
www.advbookstore.com